F. Stemmerik

Media, 15 – 7 –'13

TILL I END MY SONG

ALSO BY HAROLD BLOOM

The Anatomy of Influence

Fallen Angels

American Religious Poems: An Anthology

Jesus and Yahweh: The Names Divine

Where Shall Wisdom Be Found?

The Art of Reading Poetry

The Best Poems of the English Language: From Chaucer Through Frost

Hamlet: Poem Unlimited

Genius: A Mosaic of One Hundred Exemplary Creative Minds

Stories and Poems for Extremely Intelligent Children of All Ages

How to Read and Why

Shakespeare: The Invention of the Human

Omens of Millennium

The Western Canon

The American Religion

The Book of J

Ruin the Sacred Truths

Poetics of Influence

The Strong Light of the Canonical

Agon: Towards a Theory of Revisionism

The Breaking of the Vessels

The Flight to Lucifer: A Gnostic Fantasy

Wallace Stevens: The Poems of Our Climate

Figures of Capable Imagination

Poetry and Repression

Kabbalah and Criticism

A Map of Misreading

The Anxiety of Influence: A Theory of Poetry

The Ringers in the Tower: Studies in Romantic Tradition

Yeats

The Complete Poetry and Prose of William Blake (commentary)

Blake's Apocalypse

The Visionary Company

Shelley's Mythmaking

TILL I END MY SONG

A Gathering of Last Poems

EDITED WITH COMMENTARIES BY

Harold Bloom

HARPER

An Imprint of HarperCollins*Publishers*
www.harpercollins.com

HarperCollins books may be purchased for educational, business, or
sales promotional use. For information please write: Special Markets Department,
HarperCollins Publishers, 10 East 53rd Street, New York, NY 10022.

An extension of this copyright appears on pages 373–76.

FIRST EDITION

Designed by Jennifer Ann Daddio / Bookmark Design & Media Inc.

Library of Congress Cataloging-in-Publication Data

Till I end my song : a gathering of last poems / edited with comentaries by Harold
Bloom. — 1st ed.
    p. cm.
  ISBN 978-0-06-192305-0
  1. Poetry—History and criticism.   2. Poetics.   I. Bloom, Harold.
  PN1111.T55 2010
  809.1—dc22

                                                                    2010020773

            10 11 12 13 14 WBC/RRD 10 9 8 7 6 5 4 3 2 1

CONTENTS

INTRODUCTION

There are three kinds of "last poems" in this anthology. Some literally are the final poems these women and men composed. Others were intended to mark the end, though the poet survived a while longer and continued to work. A third group consists of poems that seem to me an imaginative conclusion to a poetic career. With all three kinds I have made an aesthetic judgment: everything in this volume is here because of its artistic excellence.

By definition, all living poets are excluded from this book. Myself seventy-nine years of age, I grieve still for many of these poets who were my friends. But knowledge, not pathos, is my purpose in gathering this anthology. Lastness is a part of knowing.

How to represent the greatest of poets? *The Tempest* proved not to be William Shakespeare's last play. But his friends and fellow actors, who put together the First Folio in 1623, seven years after his death, chose to lead off the book with *The Tempest,* which they regarded as a comedy. All through the nineteenth century and early twentieth century, common readers heard in Prospero's farewell to his magical art an intimation of Shakespeare's abandonment of the creation of shadows of reality for the stage. I stand with the common auditor and I hear in

Prospero's measured leave-taking the overtones of Shakespeare's voluntary departure.

John Milton, second in splendor only to Shakespeare, has no final lyric or overt elegy for the self, but I tend to disbelieve scholars who date *Samson Agonistes* as an earlier Miltonic work (1647–1653), since they present only unimaginative surmises. The traditional dating (1666–1670) seems to me consonant with the spirit and temper of this dark dramatic poem, most of which reads to me as having been composed after *Paradise Lost*. In May 1659, the blind poet went into hiding to escape the furies of the royalist Restoration. Arrested in October, he was released only in mid-December, and the ordeal had to have been considerable.

Triumph and tragedy fuse in *Samson Agonistes*. Even if it first was drafted in 1647, we can assume recasting well after the death of Cromwell, whose poet fell upon evil days, hemmed about by vengeful enemies. In effect, *Samson Agonistes* is Milton's last poem, and Manoa's heroic refusal to lament his son finds a legitimate place in this book.

Last poems by no means are to be identified with death poems, though the genres (to call them that) overlap. Strong poems are composed against death though not against dying. My distinction reflects the influence upon me of the sage Epicurus and of his poetic disciple, Lucretius. There is a Lucretian tradition of poetry in English, which proceeds from John Dryden on to Percy Bysshe Shelley and Lord Byron, and then emerges from repression in Alfred Lord Tennyson's dramatic monologue *Lucretius*, before passing on to Algernon Charles Swinburne, and then culminating in the Americans Walt Whitman and Wallace Stevens. The Epicurean critic Walter Pater, though dismissed by T. S. Eliot, became the hidden source of literary modernism—James Joyce, Ezra Pound, Virginia Woolf, Eliot himself, and overwhelmingly W. B. Yeats and Hart Crane.

Epicurus and Lucretius had many ambitions, but the largest was to free us from fears of death, which for them in itself was nothing at all. Liberated from heaven and hell, purgatory and limbo, we were to benefit from the demythologizing of death, be it magnified by pagans or by Christians. Dying comes to all, but "death" to no one. What Stevens called "the mythology of modern death" seems to have little force in the twenty-first century, which follows the century of the Holocaust and of other unforgivable barbarities. In so bad a time, when nations and religions alike begin to seem organized incoherences, Lucretian poems are refreshing in their difference.

The central image for freedom in Lucretius is the *clinamen* or sudden "swerve." As the atoms in the cosmos fall downward and outward they capriciously swerve, and this change in direction provides for our freedom of will. Last poems, as I read them, execute clinamens in regard to a previous poetic career. They assert a final freedom for the imagination even when they are death poems. "Death poems," as a term, is oxymoronic. As Yeats said, there is always a phantasmagoria, however desperate or extreme.

2

I turn to Yeats as an illumination of the immutable paradox of last poems. Of the group generally regarded as Yeats's death poems, two seem among his finest, *Cuchulain Comforted* (included in this book) and *Man and the Echo*. Equally powerful is the very late *The Circus Animals' Desertion*, but that is not a death poem. Much weaker are the "official" self-epitaphs, *Under Ben Bulben* and *The Black Tower*. The very last poem was a slight effusion, *Politics*, in which the impending Second World War is brushed aside at the sight of a girl:

But O that I were young again
And held her in my arms.

The sentiment is universal and admirable but does not require voicing by the major European poet of the twentieth century. Since I comment very fully on *Cuchulain Comforted* in my headnote to Yeats, I look elsewhere for his magnificence at conveying lastness. All through the poems of 1938 and 1939, he mingles a persuasive vision of a lifetime of highest service to the lyric Muse with vehement disclosures of his ongoing social attitudes. Highborn, reckless horsemen and properly respectful peasants are lauded, while the "base-born" commercial class are consigned by scorn to be ground under by what seems a violent, Fascist social order, which shall enforce eugenic cleansing. Few current readers of Yeats are much moved by these hymns to "the indomitable Irishry," and simply shrug off such aristocratic pretensions. "Arrogance and hatred are the wares," Yeats tells us, "peddled in the thoroughfares" in contrast to the "innocence and beauty born" out of "custom and ceremony." A deep lover of Yeats's poetry has to accept that this nonsense nevertheless helped produce the memorable vision of *The Second Coming:* "And everywhere the ceremony of innocence is drowned." Of the *Last Poems* of Yeats, *Man and the Echo* and *The Circus Animals' Desertion* dismiss all such claptrap, while *Cuchulain Comforted* can be read in the manner of Conor Cruise O'Brien, who found in that great poem a prophecy of the death of Fascism. Yeats flirted with the Irish Fascists and allowed himself to call Mussolini "a very great man," yet the Romantic heritage of William Blake and of Shelley finally prevailed and Yeats evaded Fascism. Unlike T. S. Eliot, Ezra Pound, and Wyndham Lewis, Yeats rejected anti-Semitism, a spiritual disease repudiated more firmly by James Joyce and by Samuel Beckett.

3

Devoutly Christian poets confront the same problems in composing last poems that all devotional verse must surmount: where faith is fixed, how much space remains for invention? Dr. Samuel Johnson argued: "The good and evil of eternity are too ponderous for the wings of wit. The mind sinks under them, content with calm belief and humble adoration." Though I welcome the best of devotional poetry, it is rarely achieved.

John Donne, dean of St. Paul's, and not the youthful libertine of *Songs and Sonnets,* is a grand exception, and is represented here by his sublime last poem, *A Hymn to God the Father.* T. S. Eliot and W. H. Auden, neo-Christian by conversion, are not at their best in devotional verse, and find their place in this book with secular finalities. Gerard Manley Hopkins composes a last poem to his closest friend, the laureate Robert Bridges, but the burden is a paean to the lost, Keatsian inspiration.

When I stand back to reflect upon these hundred poems, ranging in time from Edmund Spenser, who died in 1599, to recently dead friends and acquaintances, including A. R. Ammons, Anthony Hecht, Kenneth Koch, and James Merrill, among others, my first impression is variety. Perhaps all authentic strong poems are "last" in that the intrinsic purpose of each is to make the next poem by the same poet possible. The inner paradox of lastness is the undersong: "Let this be the next to the last!"

A number of superb poets are not represented in this anthology because I could not locate in them a distinguished last poem in any of my three senses. These included Chaucer, Sir Thomas Wyatt, Robert Burns, and a number of twentieth-century figures, Ezra Pound and Marianne Moore among others. T. S. Eliot wrote little after *Four Quartets,* but the predawn encounter with "a familiar compound ghost" in *Little Gidding,* after a London air raid, seems to me his strongest achievement, a final formulation of his life's work. Its aesthetic dignity entitles it to be Eliot's last poem.

4

At the end of the twenty-first century's initial decade, I am haunted by previous defenses of poetry—Sir Philip Sidney's and Shelley's—even as I gather this anthology, which is yet another defense. Contemporary American poetry in 2010 seems to me astonishingly rich. Such masters as Richard Wilbur, John Ashbery, W. S. Merwin, John Hollander,

Mark Strand, Jay Wright, and Louise Glück are being joined by younger poets: Anne Carson, Henri Cole, and Rosanna Warren, among others. A country that has brought forth Walt Whitman, Emily Dickinson, Robert Frost, Wallace Stevens, T. S. Eliot, Hart Crane, and Elizabeth Bishop has enjoyed a rich tradition of poetry that James Merrill, A. R. Ammons, and John Ashbery have continued. These ten are foremost (in my judgment), but any skilled reader might enumerate another ten as supplement.

The poems of our climate may seem singularly exposed in the computer age, when the sun starts to go down upon the cosmos of the printed book. We hold on to the highest poetry out of desperate need. Shakespeare invented all of us, in the sense that we now notice what always had been there, but could not have seen without him. None of our poets, not even Walt Whitman, rivals Shakespeare, and yet Whitman's influence upon the best minds and spirits of his nation remains prodigal. Ralph Waldo Emerson was the mind of America, Whitman its story of the self, inchoate yet struggling toward coherence.

The United States, Whitman proclaimed, itself was to be the greatest poem. That capacious confidence seemed irrelevant during our years in the bush, but revives in the age of Obama. Our young will yet dream their dreams, and the old (like myself) will yet see visions. If America remains an idea, then Emerson and Whitman inform that speculation, however time's revenges may darken it.

Since America is belated, and yet insists upon an earliness, our signature poem might well be Walt Whitman's vision of himself as the American Adam:

As Adam early in the morning,
Walking forth from the bower refresh'd with sleep,
Behold me where I pass, hear my voice, approach,
Touch me, touch the palm of your hand to my body as I pass,
Be not afraid of my body.

The speaker sounds like the risen Jesus of the Gnostic Gospel of Thomas, not available for Whitman to have read, but he was too much in its spirit to need its text. Whitman presents himself as the Hermetic God-Man, author of the American Bible. He inaugurated American poetry as we and the world now recognize it. At once the earliest and the last Western poetry, our native strain redefines lastness. The first American poem chosen by me for this anthology is Ralph Waldo Emerson's *Terminus*, a last poem only in theme, since it was published in 1867 and the Sage of Concord died in 1882, a few weeks before what would have been his seventy-ninth birthday. He had been falling away for a decade into senility, and *Terminus* was a shrewd prophecy of his long decline:

> Fancy departs: no more invent,
> Contract thy firmament
> To compass of a tent.
> There's not enough for this and that
> Make thy option which of two . . .
> Economize the failing river . . .

The accents of farewell in Whitman are more sonorously plangent:

> Let me glide noiselessly forth;
> With the keys of softness unlock the locks—with a whisper,
> Set ope the doors O soul.

That is Whitman in 1868, only forty-nine and with twenty-four years still to live. Elegiac forebodings belong to all poetic traditions, but what becomes peculiarly American is the self-elegy. Whitman proclaims celebration in *Song of Myself*, but his other major poems move toward lament, culminating in *When Lilacs Last in the Dooryard Bloom'd.* Its direct descendant, Eliot's *The Waste Land,* is not a dirge for European culture but an American poet's cry from the depths, recording the self's desperate stance against an Orphic *sparagmos.* Hart Crane, contesting Eliot in *The Bridge,* nevertheless knowingly repeats Whitman's lament that his Eros is crucified. Eliot's thematically last poem gives us the wonderful exchange in *Little Gidding* between a composite precursor, W. B. Yeats and Jonathan Swift dominant, and the poet learning his final lesson. Hart Crane inevitably replied in his sublime death ode, *The Broken Tower,* in which all of American Romantic tradition culminates and then is self-destroyed, to a cognitive music more absolute than any other I have heard:

> The bells, I say, the bells break down their tower
> And swing I know not where . . .

5

If your next birthday will be your eightieth, and you have read the greatest poetry all your life, then you begin to know that in the face of dying and death, the imagination is at once nothing and everything. Hamlet, the Western imagination incarnate, knows he is nothing and everything in himself, yet he is poetry itself, the center of the single, most unbelievably capacious consciousness that ever has imbued a body of literature. The Bible, Homer, Dante, Cervantes, Tolstoy, and Proust do not fade into the light of Shakespeare's dawn, but they edge toward reflecting a sun at the heart of reality. My assertion merely attempts to describe a generic experience of readership. All of Shakespeare together forms the Last Poem upon which we rely even as we forget the terms of our dependence.

A chorus in Aristophanes, favored by Kierkegaard, tells us: "You get too much at last of everything: of sunsets, of cabbages, of love." It may be that the reader of this anthology will get too much at last of last poems and yet (granted my triple sense of the genre) they are endlessly varied: from Spenser to my late friends, Vicki Hearne and Agha Shahid Ali, both of whom died in 2001. Poets may wish to observe a truce but the Furies make no bargains. For those who write sublimely well, oblivion is not to be hired.

American poets keep going down to the shoreline to struggle with their daemons. That again is the prevalence of Walt Whitman, hearing the word of death whispering out of the cradle endlessly rocking, and ebbing with the ocean of life. Wallace Stevens, T. S. Eliot, Hart Crane, Elizabeth Bishop, May Swenson, A. R. Ammons, James Wright, Amy Clampitt, Jean Garrigue, and others in this book all composed marvelous beach meditations, fragments shored against their ruins, but usually at earlier crises and not as last poems.

The late William Empson, disturbing poet and major critic, remarked to me once that Hart Crane had come to fascinate him because Crane wrote each poem as though it could be the last of his life. Investing everything in his art, Crane died when he believed (wrongly) that poetry was dead in him. Though Crane was perhaps the last American High Romantic poet, brother and peer to Shelley and Arthur Rimbaud, like them he was emotionally self-destructive. In a good sense there are no last poems, except for the singular chance of a figure closing out a tradition, and such a phenomenon is very rare, a titan like Victor Hugo or a poetic sport like Gerard Manley Hopkins. Most apparent innovators resemble T. S. Eliot, an ultimate continuator of the Romanticism he sought to overturn. In the most demanding literature, all strong rebellion is destined to be merely usurpation followed by a freshening of tradition.

6

We turn to last poems at whatever age because we both desire and fear finalities. We want to know and not know the extent of our temporal spans, and we hope to learn from the poets not how to die but how to stand against uncertainty. Montaigne, first and best of essayists, advises us to waste no energy learning how to die. When the time comes, we will know how to do it well enough.

Poems are created to last, though relatively few can achieve permanence. Most are fated to become period pieces at best. They prove to be shadows, not substantial things. Shakespeare used the word "shadows" in many senses, of which the most striking is a stage representation or role for an actor. Macbeth, recoiling from his wife's death, says life itself is a walking shadow, a poor player strutting and fretting his hour upon the stage, and then is heard no more. Last poems pragmatically rebel against that persuasive metaphor: they desire to be heard until earth's final hour, beyond the life of the individual poet.

Shakespeare's detachment, in plays and poems alike, prevents us from knowing his deep inwardness. Since he himself invented, if not inwardness itself, the most successful representations of inwardness yet achieved, we never will know how he came to accept or make friends with the necessity of dying. Was he Protestant or Catholic, moderate believer or skeptic, heretical hermetist or inaugural nihilist? Contemplating Hamlet, Lear, Othello, Macbeth, and Cleopatra and their tragedies, I come to a provisional conclusion. The rest is silence because the end *is* silence and nothing but silence.

For the late Amy Clampitt, a poet I knew and revered, at the close a silence *opens*. She was too wise to literalize her own metaphor. Silence is an attribute of lastness. Reflecting upon the poems gathered in this volume, I marvel at how many speak silence and wash our dusk with silver. Conrad Aiken, whom I met only once, was a superb poet; he is now long neglected, but his best poems abide in my memory:

Then came I to the shoreless shore of silence,
Where never summer was nor shade of tree,
Nor sound of water, nor sweet light of sun,

But only nothing and the shore of nothing,
Above, below, around, and in my heart;

Preludes for Memnon XXXIII

A Lucretian poet—like Shelley, Whitman, and Stevens—Aiken
haunts "the shoreless shore of silence," threshold to the abyss of noth-
ingness. He differs, if at all, from most poets in *Till I End My Song* by
making finely explicit his cosmic nihilism. You can regard Aiken as the
American Swinburne, provided you detach the actual Swinburne from
the current neglect he shares with Aiken. Lucretian nihilists like Swin-
burne and Edward Fitzgerald's transfigured Omar Khayyám move us
because they speak to a reality we want to evade but cannot, Freud's rea-
lity principle. To read last poems is to participate in reality testing, even
if you are a believing Christian, submissive Muslim, or trusting Jew.

7

How are we to get at the meanings of last poems? My headnotes suggest
ways of apprehending and comprehending each one in turn, but I am
wary of method. There is no method but yourself, once you have read
widely and deeply, opening yourself to the sounds and silences of the
best poetry. After well more than half a century of teaching superb stu-
dents the art of reading poetry, I begin to understand that the purpose
of teaching is to extend the blessing of more life. Even at their most
skeptical or despairing, the poems in this book intimate a time without
boundaries, though that time is a fiction of duration, the illuminated
space of the poem.

   I once thought that I read so many books because I could not meet and
speak with enough people. But by now I may have taught some twenty-five
thousand students, enough to people a small city, and still I read day and

night. Gertrude Stein wonderfully said that one writes for oneself and for strangers. One reads for oneself, but teaches others, and many do not remain strangers. Reading, teaching, and writing are for me three words for the one act of the mind. Stevensian terms fit this best: this composite act quests to find what will suffice.

Last poems by themselves will not suffice. Only *The Tempest*, viewed as a last poem, might assuage the adverting mind. There are other supreme acts of the mind in this book in addition to Shakespeare's: *Samson Agonistes*, Pope's *The Dunciad*, Shelley's *The Triumph of Life*, Lawrence's *Shadows*, Crane's *The Broken Tower*, and Merrill's *Days of 1994*, among others. All these destroy illusions, dismiss immediate survival, and yet reach out to others and otherness. The use of last poems is to propound the perpetual possibility of the self, fated to dissolve, living on in the minds and the hearts of those remaining.

No one not far from eighty relishes the forms and accents of farewell. Yet, for the secular, who reject illusion, where else is consolation to be found? In the view of its gatherer, this volume does not propose any exaltation of the spirit, but I am a critic and teacher, not a poet. Intimations of immortality collide with resigned skepticisms throughout this book. Confronting illness, pain, and dying, we learn quickly that eloquence is not enough. Neither are even the most authentic poems of consolation. Still, the beauty and wisdom of these poems reverberate into the coming silence.

—HAROLD BLOOM
June 2010

TILL I END MY SONG

EDMUND SPENSER 1552–1599

Prothalamion

K nown as "the Prince of Poets in his time," Spenser remained the poets' poet from John Milton through W. B. Yeats, a role that the archpoet Yeats has played ever since. A lifelong lover of Spenser's poetry, I regret that Elizabeth I's laureate is now read mostly by scholars, since his epic romance, *The Faerie Queene,* is both beautiful and difficult.

We do not know precisely when Spenser wrote his "last poem," in any sense of that term. He had sojourned in British-occupied Ireland as a civil servant of the religio-military Protestant ascendancy there. Burned out by the properly rebellious Irish, Spenser would return to London to beseech the Queen for preferment, a fruitless and bitter idling, as his superb *Prothalamion* (betrothal ode before a wedding) indicates in its first stanza:

When I whom sullein care,
Through discontent of my long fruitlesse stay
In Princes Court, and expectation vayne
Of idle hopes, which still doe fly away,
Like empty shaddowes, did afflict my brayne,

Walkt forth to ease my payne
Along the shoare of silver streaming *Themmes.*

To be sullen in the sweet air is the sin of *acedia,* hopeless malady
from Dante's *Inferno* on to William Wordsworth's *Intimations of Immortality* ode. Spenser, acutely conscious of this psychic danger, catches
immediately, in the poem's refrain, the precarious balance reached by his
life and his art:

Against the Brydale day, which is not long:
Sweete *Themmes* runne softly till I end my Song.

Sometimes I reflect, with amiable irony, that T. S. Eliot's *The Waste
Land* has no more eloquent line than the one he appropriates from
Spenser. A prothalamion is a spousal verse or betrothal ode, presaging a
wedding. Spenser, who had followed the Earl of Leicester before he
ceased to be Elizabeth I's favorite, transferred his loyalty to the new favorite, the Earl of Essex. To please Essex, he composed his prothalamion for the double marriages of the daughters of the Earl of Worcester,
a close friend of Essex.

Throughout the poem, Spenser counterpoints against the joyous
myth of river marriage his dark undersong of mutabilities: personal sorrows, the fall of Leicester, the past decay of the Templar order of knights.
This darkness is overcome by the illumination of the coming marriages
and the advancing greatness of Essex (stanza 9). Very subtly, the poem's
refrain promises joy in its first line and hints at coming troubles for the
poet in the second. In less than three years the Irish rebellion sent him
back to London, where he died at forty-seven, perhaps in want. As a last
poem, *Prothalamion* prophesies Spenser's unhappy close and sets the
theme for this volume: *Till I End My Song.*

Prothalamion

1

Calme was the day, and through the trembling ayre,
Sweete breathing *Zephyrus* did softly play
A gentle spirit, that lightly did delay
Hot *Titans* beames, which then did glyster fayre:
5   When I whom sullein care,
Through discontent of my long fruitlesse stay
In Princes Court, and expectation vayne
Of idle hopes, which still doe fly away,
Like empty shaddowes, did aflict my brayne,
10 Walkt forth to ease my payne
Along the shoare of silver streaming *Themmes.*
Whose rutty Bancke, the which his River hemmes,
Was paynted all with variable flowers,
And all the meades adornd with daintie gemmes,
15 Fit to decke maydens bowres,
And crowne their Paramours,
Against the Brydale day, which is not long:
    Sweete *Themmes* runne softly, till I end my Song.

2

There, in a Meadow, by the Rivers side,
20 A Flocke of *Nymphes* I chaunced to espy,
All lovely Daughters of the Flood thereby,
With goodly greenish locks all loose untyde,
As each had bene a Bryde.
And each one had a little wicker basket,
25 Made of fine twigs entrayled curiously,
In which they gathered flowers to fill their flasket:
And with fine Fingers, cropt full feateously

The tender stalkes on hye.
Of every sort, which in that Meadow grew,
30   They gathered some; the Violet pallid blew,
The little Dazie, that at evening closes,
The virgin Lillie, and the Primrose trew,
With store of vermeil Roses,
To decke their Bridegromes posies,
35   Against the Brydale day, which was not long:
     Sweete *Themmes* runne softly, till I end my Song.

     3

With that I saw two Swannes of goodly hewe,
Come softly swimming downe along the Lee;
Two fairer Birds I yet did never see:
40   The snow which doth the top of *Pindus* strew,
Did never whiter shew,
Nor *Jove* himselfe when he a Swan would be
For love of *Leda,* whiter did appeare:
Yet *Leda* was they say as white as he,
45   Yet not so white as these, nor nothing neare;
So purely white they were,
That even the gentle streame, the which them bare,
Seem'd foule to them, and bad his billowes spare
To wet their silken feathers, least they might
50   Soyle their fayre plumes with water not so fayre,
And marre their beauties bright,
That shone as heavens light,
Against their Brydale day, which was not long:
     Sweete *Themmes* runne softly, till I end my Song.

     4

55   Eftsoones the *Nymphes,* which now had Flowers their fill,
Ran all in haste, to see that silver brood,

As they came floating on the Christal Flood,
Whom when they sawe, they stood amazed still,
Their wondring eyes to fill,
60   Them seem'd they never saw a sight so fayre,
Of Fowles so lovely, that they sure did deeme
Them heavenly borne, or to be that same payre
Which through the Skie draw *Venus* silver Teeme,
For sure they did not seeme
65   To be begot of any earthly Seede,
But rather Angels or of Angels breede:
Yet were they bred of *Somers-heat* they say,
In sweetest Season, when each Flower and weede
The earth did fresh aray,
70   So fresh they seem'd as day,
Even as their Brydale day, which was not long:
    Sweete *Themmes* runne softly till I end my Song.

    5

Then forth they all out of their baskets drew,
Great store of Flowers, the honour of the field,
75   That to the sense did fragrant odours yield,
All which upon those goodly Birds they threw,
And all the Waves did strew,
That like old *Peneus* Waters they did seeme,
When downe along by pleasant *Tempes* shore
80   Scattred with Flowres, through *Thessaly* they streeme,
That they appeare through Lillies plenteous store,
Like a Brydes Chamber flore:
Two of those *Nymphes,* meane while, two Garlands bound,
Of freshest Flowres which in that Mead they found,
85   The which presenting all in trim Array,
Their snowie Foreheads therewithall they crownd,
Whil'st one did sing this Lay,

Prepar'd against that Day,
Against their Brydale day, which was not long:
90 Sweete *Themmes* runne softly till I end my Song.

6

Ye gentle Birdes, the worlds faire ornament,
And heavens glorie, whom this happie hower
Doth leade unto your lovers blisfull bower,
Joy may you have and gentle hearts content
95 Of your loves couplement:
And let faire *Venus,* that is Queene of love,
With her heart-quelling Sonne upon you smile,
Whose smile they say, hath vertue to remove
All Loves dislike, and friendships faultie guile
100 For ever to assoile.
Let endlesse Peace your steadfast hearts accord,
And blessed Plentie wait upon your bord,
And let your bed with pleasures chast abound,
That fruitfull issue may to you afford,
105 Which may your foes confound,
And make your joyes redound,
Upon your Brydale day, which is not long:
Sweete *Themmes* run softly, till I end my Song.

7

So ended she; and all the rest around
110 To her redoubled that her undersong,
Which said, their bridale daye should not be long,
And gentle Eccho from the neighbour ground,
Their accents did resound.
So forth those joyous Birdes did passe along,
115 Adowne the Lee, that to them murmurde low,

As he would speake, but that he lackt a tong,
Yeat did by signes his glad affection show,
Making his streame run slow.
And all the foule which in his flood did dwell
120 Gan flock about these twaine, that did excell
The rest, so far, as *Cynthia* doth shend
The lesser starres. So they enranged well,
Did on those two attend,
And their best service lend,
125 Against their wedding day, which was not long:
  Sweete *Themmes* run softly, till I end my song.

       8

At length they all to mery *London* came,
To mery London, my most kyndly Nurse,
That to me gave this Lifes first native sourse:
130 Though from another place I take my name,
An house of auncient fame.
There when they came, whereas those bricky towres,
The which on *Themmes* brode aged backe doe ryde,
Where now the studious Lawyers have their bowers,
135 There whylome wont the Templer Knights to byde,
Till they decayd through pride:
Next whereunto there standes a stately place,
Where oft I gayned giftes and goodly grace
Of that great Lord, which therein wont to dwell.
140 Whose want too well, now feeles my freendles case:
But Ah here fits not well
Olde woes but joyes to tell
Against the bridale daye which is not long:
  Sweete *Themmes* runne softly till I end my Song.

9

145 Yet therein now doth lodge a noble Peer,
   Great *Englands* glory and the Worlds wide wonder,
   Whose dreadfull name, late through all *Spaine* did thunder,
   And *Hercules* two pillors standing neere,
   Did make to quake and feare:
150 Faire branch of Honor, flower of Chevalrie,
   That fillest *England* with thy triumphes fame,
   Joy have thou of thy noble victorie,
   And endlesse happinesse of thine owne name
   That promiseth the same:
155 That through thy prowesse and victorious armes,
   Thy country may be freed from forraine harmes:
   And great *Elisaes* glorious name may ring
   Through al the world, fil'd with thy wide Alarmes,
   Which some brave muse may sing
160 To ages following,
   Upon the Brydale day, which is not long:
      Sweete *Themmes* runne softly till I end my Song.

10

   From those high Towers, this noble Lord issuing,
   Like Radiant *Hesper* when his golden hayre
165 In th'*Ocean* billowes he hath Bathed fayre,
   Descended to the Rivers open vewing,
   With a great traine ensuing.
   Above the rest were goodly to bee seene
   Two gentle Knights of lovely face and feature
170 Beseeming well the bower of anie Queene,
   With gifts of wit and ornaments of nature,
   Fit for so goodly stature:
   That like the twins of *Jove* they seem'd in sight,
   Which decke the Bauldricke of the Heavens bright.

175 They two forth pacing to the Rivers side,
   Received those two faire Brides, their Loves delight,
   Which at th'appointed tyde,
   Each one did make his Bryde,
   Against their Brydale day, which is not long:
180   Sweete *Themmes* runne softly, till I end my Song.

From *The Ocean to Cynthia*

R alegh can seem to be an improbable historical personage: politician, courtier, warrior, adventurer, explorer, historian, great but throwaway poet. We remember him as the founder of the first colony in Virginia and as the friend and patron of Edmund Spenser and other poets. A charismatic personality, Ralegh was doom-eager. Elizabeth's favorite from 1583 to 1592, he fell from her grace for debauching her maids of honor. His lament, *The Ocean to Cynthia,* is a plea to be taken back again. Spenser in *The Faerie Queene* had allegorized Ralegh as the Shepherd of the Ocean, and Elizabeth as Cynthia (Artemis), virgin goddess of the moon and governor of the ocean's tides.

In and out of Elizabeth's indulgence after 1592, Ralegh suffered greatly under James I, who imprisoned him in the Tower of London for thirteen years, and then had him beheaded on a false charge of treason.

Of Ralegh's great chant, *The Ocean to Cynthia,* one should observe that it constitutes an elegy for his entire career and an accurate prophecy of his persecution by King James. It is a last poem in the sense that it catches up the great theme of his life, and is a broken monument of his great desires.

I have retained the original spelling here, as with Spenser. Both poets cultivated an archaic atmosphere and stance, and modernizing the spelling loses much of their flavor.

From *The Ocean to Cynthia*

XXIV

THE 11TH: AND LAST BOOKE OF THE OCEAN TO SCINTHIA

Sufficeth it to yow my ioyes interred,
In simpell wordes that I my woes cumplayne,
Yow that then died when first my fancy erred,
Ioyes vnder dust that never live agayne.

5 If to the liuinge weare my muse adressed,
Or did my minde her own spirrit still inhold,
Weare not my livinge passion so repressed,
As to the dead, the dead did thes vnfold,

Sume sweeter wordes, sume more becumming vers,
10 Should wittness my myshapp in hygher kynd,
But my loues wounds, my fancy in the hearse,
The Idea but restinge, of a wasted minde,

The blossumes fallen, the sapp gon from the tree,
The broken monuments of my great desires,
15 From thes so lost what may th' affections bee,
What heat in Cynders of extinguisht fiers?

Lost in the mudd of thos hygh flowinge streames
Which through more fayrer feilds ther courses bend,
Slayne with sealf thoughts, amasde in fearfull dreams,
20 Woes without date, discumforts without end,

From frutfull trees I gather withred leues
And glean the broken eares with misers hands,
Who sumetyme did inioy the waighty sheves
I seeke faire floures amidd the brinish sand.

25 All in the shade yeven in the faire soon dayes
Vnder thos healthless trees I sytt alone,
Wher joyfull byrdds singe neather lovely layes
Nor Phillomen recounts her direfull mone.

No feedinge flockes, no sheapherds cumpunye
30 That might renew my dollorus consayte,
While happy then, while loue and fantasye
Confinde my thoughts onn that faire flock to waite;

No pleasinge streames fast to the ocean wendinge
The messengers sumetymes of my great woe,
35 But all onn yearth as from the colde stormes bendinge
Shrinck from my thoughts in hygh heauens and below.

Oh hopefull loue my obiect, and invention,
Oh, trew desire the spurr of my consayte,
Oh, worthiest spirrit, my minds impulsion,
40 Oh, eyes transpersant, my affections bayte,

Oh, princely forme, my fancies adamande,
Deuine consayte, my paynes acceptance,
Oh, all in onn, oh heaven on yearth transparant,
The seat of ioyes, and loues abundance!

45 Out of that mass of mirakells, my Muse,
Gathered thos floures, to her pure sences pleasinge,

Out of her eyes (the store of ioyes) did chuse
Equall delights, my sorrowes counterpoysinge.

Her regall lookes, my rigarus sythes suppressed,
50   Small dropes of ioies, sweetned great worlds of woes,
One gladsume day a thowsand cares redressed.
Whom Loue defends, what fortune overthrowes?

When shee did well, what did ther elce amiss?
When shee did ill what empires could haue pleased?
55   No other poure effectinge wo, or bliss,
Shee gave, shee tooke, shee wounded, shee apeased.

The honor of her loue, Loue still devisinge,
Woundinge my mind with contrary consayte,
Transferde it sealf sumetyme to her aspiringe
60   Sumetyme the trumpett of her thoughts retrayt;

To seeke new worlds, for golde, for prayse, for glory,
To try desire, to try loue seuered farr,
When I was gonn shee sent her memory
More stronge then weare ten thowsand shipps of warr,

65   To call mee back, to leue great honors thought,
To leue my frinds, my fortune, my attempte,
To leue the purpose I so longe had sought
And holde both cares, and cumforts in contempt.

Such heat in Ize, such fier in frost remaynde,
70   Such trust in doubt, such cumfort in dispaire,
Mich like the gentell Lamm, though lately waynde,
Playes with the dug though finds no cumfort ther.

But as a boddy violently slayne
Retayneath warmth although the spirrit be gonn,
75   And by a poure in nature moves agayne
Till it be layd below the fatall stone; . . .

SIR PHILIP SIDNEY (1554–1586)

From *Astrophel and Stella:* "Who will in fairest book"

Sidney was the fulfillment of an English humanist ideal: a powerful aristocrat, courtly lover, suave diplomat, gallant warrior, committed Protestant, classical rhetorician, major poet, and above all master of *sprezzatura,* the graceful carelessness of the highborn who are immensely gifted amateurs of everything. Mortally wounded in Holland fighting against Spain, he gave his canteen to a dying soldier, saying: "Your need is greater than mine."

He wrote no death poem, and I have chosen a sonnet from the famous sequence completed four years before his death. When both were young, he had been betrothed to Penelope Rich, daughter of the Earl of Essex. Sidney is Astrophel (star lover) and she Stella (star) in a Petrarchan sequence reflecting an authentic passion. In the marvelous Sonnet LXXI ("Who will in fairest book of Nature know"), he celebrates his Penelope as "that inward sun" (reason) whose eyes repel "those night-birds" (vices) and guides him also to "virtue." The magnificent last line does not reverse this idealization but balances it: "But, oh, Desire still cries, 'Give me some food.'"

The betrothal was broken, and Penelope unhappily married Lord

Rich. Since Sidney's uncle was the Earl of Leicester, unfortunate favorite of Queen Elizabeth before the equally unfortunate Earl of Essex rose and fell in her regard, it is highly possible that a marriage between the houses of Leicester and Essex proved politically inexpedient, in the judgment of Elizabeth and her counselors.

"Who will in fairest book"

LXXI

Who will in fairest book of Nature know
How virtue may best lodged in beauty be,
Let him but learn of love to read in thee,
Stella, those fair lines which true goodness show.
5 There shall he find all vices' overthrow,
Not by rude force, but sweetest sovereignty
Of reason, from whose light those night-birds fly,
That inward sun in thine eyes shineth so,
And, not content to be perfection's heir
10 Thyself, dost strive all minds that way to move,
Who mark in thee what is in thee most fair.
So while thy beauty draws the heart to love,
    As fast thy virtue bends that love to good.
    But, ah, Desire still cries, "Give me some food."

"Down in the depth of mine iniquity"

Close friend and biographer of Sidney, Greville became Chancellor of the Exchequer under James I. He wrote few or no poems during the last three decades of his life and published nothing. *Caelica* ("heavenly one") was printed five years after his death. A volume of strong poems, frequently devotional, it is best when a throwback to Tudor "plain style," rejecting Petrarchan influence. I give "Down in the depth of mine iniquity," a poem he could have regarded as his "last," since its concern is with the Christian Four Last Things. Somber and precise, Greville seems a foreshadowing of John Donne's *Divine Poems*. The reader should compare this poem with Donne's *A Hymn to God the Father,* also given in this volume.

It fascinates me to compare the four couplet refrains at the end of the stanzas with one another. The first two are identical, the third simply substitutes "not divine" for "and divine," and the fourth repeats the revised third, while replacing "Even there appears this saving God of mine" with "Thus hath his death rais'd up this soul of mine." The poem throughout anticipates both Donne and George Herbert by implicitly acknowledging how difficult it is to pray sincerely. Though written long before Greville's unexpected death, it shows him ruggedly ready for anything that could transpire. In his wealthy retirement, he was stabbed to death by a long-serving retainer who feared neglect in Greville's will.

"Down in the depth of mine iniquity"

XCIX

Down in the depth of mine iniquity,
That ugly centre of infernal spirits;
Where each sin feels her own deformity,
In those peculiar torments she inherits,
    Depriv'd of human graces, and divine,
    Even there appears this saving God of mine.

And in this fatal mirror of transgression,
Shows man as fruit of his degeneration,
The error's ugly infinite impression,*
10 Which bears the faithless down to desperation;
    Depriv'd of human graces and divine,
    Even there appears this saving God of mine.

In power and truth, almighty and eternal,
Which on the sin reflects strange desolation,
With glory scourging all the sprites infernal,
And uncreated hell with unprivation;
    Depriv'd of human graces, not divine,
    Even there appears this saving God of mine.

For on this sp'ritual cross condemned lying,
20 To pains infernal by eternal doom,

---

*The error's . . . impression: As Yvor Winters has pointed out, this line is the subject of the verb "shows."

I see my Saviour for the same sins dying,
And from that hell I fear'd, to free me, come;
   Depriv'd of human graces, not divine,
    Thus hath his death rais'd up this soul of mine.

MICHAEL DRAYTON (1563–1631)

Last Verses:
"So well I love thee"

I have kept Drayton's original spelling of this very personal poem, in which he gives final expression to his lifelong, chaste love for Anne Goodeare, Lady Rainsford. A highly professional poet and a friend of William Shakespeare, Drayton began as a disciple of Edmund Spenser. Of artisan origins, the ten-year-old Drayton aspired to be a poet and became a page in the service of Sir Henry Goodeare, a friend of Sidney. Goodeare's daughter Anne and Drayton were childhood friends, but their mutual love was socially impossible and they sanely settled for a perpetual friendship. His sonnet sequence *Idea* is inspired by her, as is his last poem.

Drayton never married but had a host of friends among the writers of his day. His most ambitious poem, the vast *Poly-Olbion,* is now read only by scholars, but I admire it intensely. It is a survey of England and Wales, thirty thousand lines in length, covering vast tracts of nature, history, and legend, county by county.

His poignant *Last Verses* is a superb love poem, summing up an attachment of almost sixty years. Few other poems of farewell are this humane and quietly eloquent.

Last Verses

These verses weare made
by Michaell Drayton Esquier
Poett Lawreatt
the night before hee dyed

Soe well I love thee, as without thee I
Love nothing; yf I might chuse, I'de rather dye
Then bee on day debarde thy companye.

Since beasts, and plantes doe growe, and live and move,
5   Beastes are those men, that such a life approve:
Hee onlye lives, that deadly is in love.

The corne that in the grownd is sowen first dies
And of on seed doe manye eares arise:
Love this worldes corne, by dying multiplies.

10   The seeds of love first by thy eyes weare throwne
Into a grownd untild, a harte unknowne
To beare such fruitt, tyll by thy handes t'was sowen.

Looke as your looking glass by chance may fall
Devyde and breake in manye peyces smale
15   And yett shewes forth, the selfe same face in all;

Proportions, features, graces just the same,
And in the smalest peyce as well the name
Of fayrest one deserves, as in the richest frame.

Soe all my thoughts are peyces but of you
20 Whiche put together makes a glass soe true
As I therin noe others face but yours can veiwe.

From *Doctor Faustus*

T he son of a shoemaker, Marlowe's gifts won him a scholarship to Cambridge University. An undergraduate dramatist, he also began early on his underground career as a secret agent for the Elizabethan CIA. When he was twenty-three, his *Tamburlaine the Great* reinvented London drama, principally through Marlowe's extraordinary command of a blank verse that intoxicated audiences. William Shakespeare was part of such an audience, and it is accurate to observe that the greatest of all dramatists served an apprenticeship to Marlowe.

For all his success, Marlowe was reckless and desperate. He killed a man in a London sword fight, and acquired a reputation as a religious and sexual rebel. On May 30, 1593, he was stabbed to death in a London tavern, supposedly in a dispute about the reckoning. Since the three killers present were all secret agents, it is a fair assumption that the twenty-nine-year-old major poet-dramatist had been terminated with maximum prejudice for knowing too much.

The desire for knowledge and power is the theme of Marlowe's last play, *Doctor Faustus*. Like Marlowe's other hero-villains—Tamburlaine, the Guise, Edward II, and Barabas the Jew of Malta—the magician-scholar

Faustus is an "overreacher," and pays with his soul. This need not be interpreted as a yielding to conventional religion and morality. Anguished and despairing, Faustus in his final speech cries out: "I'll burn my books." This farewell to the magical quest for knowledge is like a confession made under torture. Marlowe, rebel to the end, stands apart from the fall of Faustus and dies by the violence he both celebrated and lived.

FAUSTUS Ah Faustus,

Now hast thou but one bare hour to live,

And then thou must be damned perpetually.

Stand still, you ever-moving spheres of heaven,

130 That time may cease and midnight never come.

Fair nature's eye, rise again, and make

Perpetual day; or let this hour be but

A year, a month, a week, a natural day,

That Faustus may repent and save his soul.

*O lente, lente, currite noctis equi!**

The stars move still, time runs, the clock will strike.

The devil will come, and Faustus must be damned.

O I'll leap up to my God! Who pulls me down?

See, see, where Christ's blood streams in the firmament!

140 One drop would save my soul, half a drop. Ah, my Christ!

Rend not my heart for naming of my Christ!

Yet will I call on him. O spare me, Lucifer!

Where is it now? 'Tis gone:

And see where God stretcheth out his arm,

And bends his ireful brows.

Mountains and hills, come, come, and fall on me,

And hide me from the heavy wrath of God.

No, no!

Then will I headlong run into the earth.

150 Earth gape! O no, it will not harbour me.

You stars that reigned at my nativity,

Whose influence hath allotted death and hell,

Now draw up Faustus like a foggy mist

Into the entrails of you labouring clouds,

---

*"O run slowly, slowly, horses of the night"; the lover who says this in Ovid, *Amores* I.xiii.40, wants to prolong the night in his mistress's arms.

That when they vomit forth into the air,

My limbs may issue from their smoky mouths,

So that* my soul may but ascend to heaven.

The watch strikes.

Ah, half the hour is passed: 'twill all be passed anon.

O God,

160 If thou wilt not have mercy on my soul,

Yet for Christ's sake, whose blood hath ransomed me,

Impose some end to my incessant pain;

Let Faustus live in hell a thousand years,

A hundred thousand, and at last be saved!

Oh, no end is limited† to damnèd souls.

Why wert thou not a creature wanting soul?

Or why is this immortal that thou hast?

Ah, Pythagoras' metempsychosis,‡ were that true

This soul should fly from me and I be changed

170 Unto some brutish beast: all beasts are happy,

For when they die

Their souls are soon dissolved in elements;

But mine must live still§ to be plagued in hell.

Cursed be the parents that engendered me!

No, Faustus, curse thyself, curse Lucifer

That hath deprived thee of the joys of heaven.

The clock striketh twelve.

It strikes, it strikes! Now body, turn to air,

Or Lucifer will bear thee quick¶ to hell!

Thunder and lightning.

*if only
†appointed
‡Pythagoras's theory that at death the soul passed into some other creature
§forever
¶alive

O soul, be changed to little water-drops
180 And fall into the ocean, ne'er be found.

Enter DEVILS.

My God, my God! Look not so fierce on me!
Adders and serpents, let me breathe awhile!
Ugly hell, gape not! Come not, Lucifer;
I'll burn my books!*—Ah, Mephostophilis!

Exeunt with him.

*of magic

From *The Tempest*

Shakespeare, greatest of all writers in human history, has no last play or last poem. Always challenging himself to surpass his forerunner Marlowe, he went beyond *Doctor Faustus* in *The Tempest* (1611), eighteen years after Marlowe's murder. Prospero the magician is an implicit critique of Faustus. Both names mean "the favored one," in Italian and Latin, respectively. Simon Magus, blamed for the Gnostic heresy by the fathers of the Church, took the cognomen of Faustus when he came to Rome.

Prospero is served by the "sprite" or angel, Ariel, while Faustus is aided and then doomed by Mephostophilis. Though Prospero speaks of drowning his magic book, we do not see him do so, and no burning of books is involved. Point by point, Prospero undoes Faustus, even as Shakespeare transcends Marlowe.

Prospero has been taken to speak for Shakespeare himself, bidding us farewell:

We are such stuff
As dreams are made on; and our little life
Is rounded with a sleep.

PROSPERO Ye elves of hills, brooks, standing lakes, and groves;
      And ye that on the sands with printless foot
      Do chase the ebbing Neptune,* and do fly him
      When he comes back; you demi-puppets that
      By moonshine do the green sour ringlets make,
      Whereof the ewe not bites; and you whose pastime
      Is to make midnight mushrooms,† that rejoice
40   To hear the solemn curfew;‡ by whose aid—
      Weak masters§ though ye be—I have bedimmed
      The noontide sun, called forth the mutinous winds,
      And 'twixt the green sea and the azured vault
      Set roaring war: to the dread rattling thunder
      Have I given fire, and rifted Jove's stout oak
      With his own bolt; the strong-based promontory
      Have I made shake, and by the spurs¶ plucked up
      The pine and cedar: graves at my command
      Have waked their sleepers, oped, and let 'em forth
50   By my so potent Art. But this rough magic
      I here abjure; and, when I have required
      Some heavenly music,—which even now I do,—
      To work mine end upon their senses, that
      This airy charm is for, I'll brake my staff,
      Bury it certain fadoms in the earth,
      And deeper than did ever plummet sound
      I'll drown my book.**

*Neptune ocean
†grow overnight, so their nurture is attributed to elves
‡After curfew tolls, spirits and elves can walk abroad.
§the magician's demonic agents
¶roots
**which is necessary to his magic

A Hymn to God the Father

D onne came from a wealthy London family and received a
Roman Catholic education, but became the Anglican dean
of St. Paul's in London. His early libertine poetry, *Songs
and Sonnets,* circulated widely in manuscript but was kept
from publication until 1633, two years after the famous preacher's death.

There is little difference in the surpassing wit of the metaphysical,
secular lyrics and the later *Divine Poems.* The hymn given here was com-
posed by Donne during a serious illness in 1623. He survived, to live
another eight years, but in spirit the lastness of this poem could hardly
be surpassed.

A Hymn to God the Father

I

Wilt thou forgive that sin where I begun,
    Which is my sin, though it were done before?
Wilt thou forgive that sin, through which I run,
    And do run still: though still I do deplore?
        When thou hast done, thou hast not done,
           For I have more.

II

Wilt thou forgive that sin which I have won
    Others to sin? and, made my sin their door?
Wilt thou forgive that sin which I did shun
A year, or two, but wallowed in a score?
        When thou hast done, thou hast not done,
           For I have more.

III

I have a sin of fear, that when I have spun
    My last thread, I shall perish on the shore;
But swear by thy self, that at my death thy son
    Shall shine as he shines now, and heretofore;
        And, having done that, thou hast done,
           I fear no more.

From *Pleasure Reconciled to Virtue*

T he son of a London bricklayer, Jonson was educated at Westminster School by the great scholar William Camden. He fought heroically in Flanders and came back to London as an actor-dramatist, receiving crucial help from Shakespeare, whose close friend he became. Jonson is a magnificent comic playwright, particularly in *Volpone* (1606), *The Alchemist* (1610), and *Bartholomew Fair* (1614). But his tragedies, *Sejanus* and *Catiline,* failed miserably. Besides his comedies, his genius manifested in his classical lyrics and epigrams, a body of poetry vastly influential throughout the seventeenth century. In his court masques, Jonson found his truest form, under the patronage of James I. Though *Pleasure Reconciled to Virtue* was composed in 1618, I give its concluding dance songs here as Jonson's last poem in the sense that his mature view finds inevitable form in this transmutation of court entertainment into high art.

Hercules, who by legend chose Virtue over Pleasure, is replaced in these concluding dance songs by Daedalus the fabulous artificer, a figure for exalted art in design, music, and Jonsonian poetry, able to reconcile aesthetic and moral concern.

HERCULES   But Hermes,* stay a little, let me pause.

  Who's this that leads?

MERCURY   A guide that gives them laws

  To all their motions: Daedalus† the wise.

HERCULES   And doth in sacred harmony comprise

  His precepts?

MERCURY   Yes.

210 HERCULES   They may securely prove‡

  Then any labyrinth, though it be of love.

Here, while they put themselves in form, DEADALUS *had his first*

SONG

  Come on, come on; and where you go,

      So interweave the curious knot,§

  As even the observer scarce may know

      Which lines are Pleasure's and which not.

  First, figure out the doubtful way

      At which awhile all youth should stay,

220 Where she and Virtue did contend

      Which should have Hercules to friend.¶

  Then, as all actions of mankind

      Are but a labyrinth or maze,

  So let your dances be entwined,

      Yet not perplex men unto gaze;**

---

*"Mercury" in Greek

†great designer and artificer who built the labyrinth for Minos; here he descends from the "hill of skill' to preside over the remainder of the masque

‡experience

§complex choreographic interweaving of lines of dancers. The masquers are literally acting out Daedalus's metaphorical instructions in this part of the masque, and it will be hard to tell pleasures and virtues apart.

¶referring to the Choice of Hercules. The episode of the Choice has happened in the past, and Hercules represents a moral being already tested.

**into bewilderment

But measured, and so numerous too,
   As men may read each act you do,
   And when they see the graces meet,
   Admire the wisdom of your feet.
230 For dancing is an exercise
   Not only shows the mover's wit,
   But maketh the beholder wise,*
   As he hath power to rise to it.

The first dance.

After which DAEDALUS *again.*

SONG 2
O more, and more; this was so well
   As praise wants half his voice to tell;
         Again yourselves compose,
240 And now put all the aptness on
   Of figure, that proportion
         Or colour can disclose—†
That if those silent arts‡ were lost,
   Design and picture, they might boast
         From you a newer ground,§
   Instructed by the heightening sense
         Of dignity and reverence
            In your true motions found:
   Begin, begin; for look, the fair
250 Do longing listen to what air¶

---

*wise: by understanding its symbolic significance
†And now . . . disclose: arrange your postures and expressions with the same skill that design and painting use
‡silent arts: architectural design and pictures are silent poetry
§ground: basis (conceptually); base (architecturally); underlaid color (in painting); bass (musically)
¶melody

You form your second touch,*
That they may vent their murmuring hymns
Just to the tune you move your limbs,
And wish their own were such.
Make haste, make haste, for this
The labyrinth of beauty is.

The second dance.

That ended, DAEDALUS.

SONG 3
260 It follows now you are to prove
The subtlest maze of all, that's love,
And if you stay too long,
The fair will think you do 'em wrong.
Go, choose among, but with a mind
As gentle as the stroking wind
Runs o'er the gentler flowers.
And so let all your actions smile,
As if they meant not be beguile
The ladies, but the hours.
270 Grace, laughter and discóurse may meet,
And yet the beauty not go less:†
For what is noble should be sweet,
But not dissolved in wantonness.
Will you‡ that I give the law
To all your sport, and sum it?§
It should be such should¶ envy draw,
But ever overcome it.

*passage of music
†be worth less
‡do you wish
§sum it up
¶that should

280 *Here they danced with the ladies, and the whole revels* followed;* *which ended,* MERCURY *called to him[†] in this following speech, which* *was after repeated in song by two trebles, two tenors, a bass, and the* *whole chorus.*

SONG 4

An eye of looking back were well,
   Or any murmur that would tell
      Your thoughts, how you were sent
          And went,
To walk with Pleasure, not to dwell.
These, these are hours by Virtue spared
   Herself, she being her own reward,
      But she will have you know
290   That though
Her sports be soft, her life is hard.
   You must return unto the hill,
      And there advance
With labour, and inhabit still
      That height and crown
From whence you ever may look down
      Upon triumphèd[‡] Chance.
She, she it is, in darkness shines.
   'Tis she that still herself refines,
300   By her own light, to every eye
More seen, more known when Vice stands by.
And though a stranger here on earth,
In heaven she hath her right of birth.
      There, there is Virtue's seat,[§]

---

[*]the part of the masque in which the "beholders" would, literally, "rise to it" and join with the masquers in the dancing, which would go on a good while
[†]Daedalus
[‡]triumphed over
[§]official place

Strive to keep her your own;
    'Tis only she can make you great,
Though place* here make you known.

*After which, they danced their last dance, and returned into the
scene, which closed and was a mountain again as before.*

*status, rank

ROBERT HERRICK (1591–1674)

The White Island,
or *Place of the Blest*

The son of a goldsmith in London, Herrick was trained in his father's craft, then went to Cambridge and became a clergyman. A disciple of Ben Jonson, Herrick became a rural minister and wrote a wealth of short poems in Jonson's classical mode. These secular poems continue to delight readers and are a permanent achievement. Only a few of Herrick's religious lyrics are so persuasive. Particularly beautiful, *The White Island* can serve as Herrick's last poem, though it was composed a quarter century before his death. He had written himself out by 1647, and the "candor" or white glow of this vision of the place of the blessed retains its glory.

The White Island, *or* Place of the Blest

In this world, the isle of dreams,
While we sit by sorrow's streams,
Tears and terrors are our themes,
           Reciting;

5 But when once from hence we fly,
More and more approaching nigh
Unto young eternity,
           Uniting

In that whiter island, where
10 Things are evermore sincere,
Candor here and lustre there
           Delighting:

There no monstrous fancies shall
Out of hell an horror call
15 To create, or cause at all,
           Affrighting.

There in calm and cooling sleep
We our eyes shall never steep,
But eternal watch shall keep,
20   Attending

Pleasures, such as shall pursue
Me immortalized, and you;
And fresh joys, as never, too,
           Have ending.

GEORGE HERBERT (1593–1633)

Love (III)

Herbert is much the best devotional poet in the language, superior even to John Donne, Henry Vaughan, Christina Rossetti, Gerard Manley Hopkins, T. S. Eliot, and W. H. Auden.

Like Andrew Marvell, Hopkins, and Emily Dickinson, Herbert chose not to publish in his lifetime.

Born to a noble family, Herbert attended Cambridge University and eventually became a rector near Salisbury. He wrote most of his poems in his final years and designed them into the shape of his posthumous volume, *The Temple*. A follower of Donne's kind of wit, Herbert subtly employed it to undermine secular love poetry. Amazingly and uniquely, Herbert hijacks amatory verse and turns it into prayer.

Love (III) is the true conclusion to *The Temple*. The concealed pretext is Luke 12:37:

Blessed are those servants, whom the lord when he cometh shall find watching: verily I say to you, that he shall gird himself, and make them to sit down to meat, and will come and serve them.

The "quick-eyed Love" contrasts the blind Cupid and the living eyes of Christian love, which illuminate the poem.

Love [III]

Love bade me welcome: yet my soul drew back,
         Guilty of dust and sin.
But quick-eyed Love, observing me grow slack
         From my first entrance in,
5   Drew nearer to me, sweetly questioning
         If I lacked any thing.

"A guest," I answered, "worthy to be here":
         Love said, "You shall be he."
"I the unkind, ungrateful? Ah, my Dear,
10   I cannot look on thee."
Love took my hand, and smiling did reply,
         "Who made the eyes but I?"

"Truth Lord, but I have marred them: let my shame
         Go, where it doth deserve."
15   "And know you not," says Love, "who bore the blame?"
         "My Dear, then I will serve."
"You must sit down," says Love, "and taste my meat":
         So I did sit and eat.

JAMES SHIRLEY (1596–1666)

Dirge

S hirley, a popular London dramatist, fought bravely for the Royalists in the Civil War. He scraped out a living teaching school in London, after Cromwell's victory. The Great Fire of London (1666) destroyed Shirley's house, and with his wife he died destitute on the streets two weeks later. He is remembered only for his powerful *Dirge* (1659), one of Robert Frost's favorite poems.

Dirge*

The glories of our blood and state
    Are shadows, not substantial things;
There is no armor against fate;
    Death lays his icy hand on kings;
5   Scepter and crown
          Must tumble down,
And in the dust be equals made
With the poor crooked scythe and spade.

Some men with swords may reap the field,
10   And plant fresh laurels where they kill;
But their strong nerves at last must yield,
    They tame but one another still;
          Early or late,
          They stoop to fate,
15 And must give up their murmuring breath,
When they, pale captives, creep to death.

The garlands wither on your brow,
    Then boast no more your mighty deeds;
Upon death's purple altar now,
20   See where the victor-victim bleeds;

*From *The Contention of Ajax and Ulysses for the Armor of Achilles* (1659) Cf. Ovid, *Metamorphoses*, XIII.I–398. This poem, Shirley's most celebrated lyric, concludes the drama.

Your heads must come
To the cold tomb;
Only the actions of the just
Smell sweet, and blossom in their dust.

Of the Last Verses
in the Book

F amous in his own time, Waller was a Royalist turncoat who
informed on his fellow conspirators, all of whom were hanged.
The morally dubious Waller got off with a year in the Tower
and banishment. After the Restoration, he flourished politi-
cally if not poetically.

Of the Last Verses concludes his *Divine Poems* (1685) and is moving
by any standards. Written when Waller was seventy-nine, my current
age, they startle me by their eloquent relevance, subdued yet expectant.
The concluding motto is from Virgil's *Fifth Eclogue:* "attired in dazzling
white he stands in wonder at Heaven's unknown threshold" (V, 56).

Of the Last Verses in the Book*

When we for age could neither read nor write,
The subject made us able to indite;
The soul, with nobler resolutions decked,
The body stooping, does herself erect.
5   No mortal parts are requisite to raise
Her that, unbodied, can her Maker praise.

The seas are quiet when the winds give o'er;
So, calm are we when passions are no more,
For then we know how vain it was to boast
10   Of fleeting things, so certain to be lost.
Clouds of affection from our younger eyes
Conceal that emptiness which age descries.

The soul's dark cottage, battered and decayed,
Lets in new light through chinks that time has made;
15   Stronger by weakness, wiser, men become,
As they draw near to their eternal home.
Leaving the old, both worlds at once they view,
That stand upon the threshold of the new.

—*Miratur Limen Olympi.*
Vergil.†

---

*I.e., of the "Divine Poems," first published in 1685.
†Cf. Vergil, *Eclogues,* v. 56: Candidus insuetum miratur limen Olympi ("Arrayed in dazzling white, he stands enraptured at Heaven's unfamiliar threshold").

JOHN MILTON (1608–1674)

From *Samson Agonistes*

M ilton, eight years old when William Shakespeare died, conceivably might have seen the dramatist on the streets of London, where the boy's father was an affluent writer of legal documents.

The young poet attended Cambridge and then spent years studying at home, absorbing all of Western tradition. Formidably learned in languages and literature, Milton toured Italy in 1638 and 1639, returning home to join what became the Cromwellean side in the civil wars. In time he became Secretary for Foreign Tongues to Cromwell's Council of State, serving from 1649 to 1655, despite his increasing blindness.

He was in danger from the Stuart Restoration in 1660, when he was imprisoned for a while as a defender of regicide, but was released. From 1660 to 1665, he dictated *Paradise Lost* and went on to compose *Paradise Regained* and to revise *Samson Agonistes*.

Manoa, Samson's father, refuses to lament his heroic son, and is answered by Milton's final chorus. The blind old poet, whose books had been burned by the public hangman, indomitably celebrates the blind Hebrew hero, with whom he identifies. It is difficult to think of Milton, a fiery prophet, ending in "calm of mind, all passion spent," but that is what he desires.

MANOA Come, come, no time for lamentation now,
    Nor much more cause; Samson hath quit himself
1710 Like Samson, and heroicly hath finished
    A life heroic, on his enemies
    Fully revenged; hath left them years of mourning,
    And lamentation to the sons of Caphtor*
    Through all Philistian bounds. To Israel
    Honour hath left, and freedom: let but them
    Find courage to lay hold on this occasion;
    To himself and father's house eternal fame;
    And, which is best and happiest yet, all this
    With God not parted from him, as was feared,
1720 But favouring and assisting to the end.
    Nothing is here for tears, nothing to wail
    Or knock the breast, no weakness, no contempt,
    Dispraise, or blame, nothing but well and fair,
    And what may quiet us in a death so noble.
    Let us go find the body where it lies
    Soaked in his enemies' blood, and from the stream
    With lavers† pure and cleansing herbs wash off
    The clotted gore. I with what speed‡ the while
    (Gaza is not in plight§ to say us nay)
1730 Will send for all my kindred, all my friends,
    To fetch him hence and solemnly attend
    With silent obsequy and funeral train
    Home to his father's house: there will I build him
    A monument, and plant it round with shade
    Of laurel ever green, and branching palm,
    With all his trophies hung, and acts enrolled

*original home of the Philistines
†basins
‡with whatever speed I can
§in condition

In copious legend, or sweet lyric song.
Thither shall all the valiant youth resort,
And from his memory inflame their breasts
1740 To matchless valour and adventures high;
The virgins also shall on feastful days
Visit his tomb with flowers, only bewailing
His lot unfortunate in nuptial choice,
From whence captivity and loss of eyes.
CHORUS All is best, though we oft doubt,
What the unsearchable dispose
Of highest wisdom brings about,
And ever best found in the close.
Oft he seems to hide his face,
1750 But unexpectedly returns
And to his faithful champion hath in place*
Bore witness gloriously; whence Gaza mourns,
And all that band them to resist
His uncontrollable intent:
His servants he, with new acquist†
Of true experience from this great event,
With peace and consolation hath dismissed,
And calm of mind, all passion spent.

*at hand
†acquisition

ANDREW MARVELL (1621–1678)

On Mr. Milton's Paradise Lost

So unique and original a poet is Marvell that he lacks all precursors and has no true descendants, though John Ashbery at times approaches being one. A statesman who served both Cromwell and the Stuart Restoration, Marvell had no interest in publishing his poetry. A friend and champion of John Milton, Marvell found admirers in the Romantic period (William Hazlitt, Charles Lamb, and Alfred, Lord Tennyson) and in the twentieth century (T. S. Eliot, William Empson, and Frank Kermode).

One of Marvell's best poems is his tribute to the 1667 first version of *Paradise Lost,* a searching celebration that raises and yet transcends the anxiety that Milton's genius will "ruin the sacred truths" of Christian tradition and replace them by "fable and old song."

Always fierce when polemical, Marvell hits at John Dryden (the "Town-Bays") and compares Milton to the blind seer Tiresias, with whom Eliot will identify himself in *The Waste Land.*

On Mr. Milton's Paradise Lost

When I beheld the Poet blind, yet bold,
In slender Book his vast Design unfold,
Messiah Crown'd, *Gods* Reconcil'd Decree,
Rebelling *Angels,* the Forbidden Tree,
5   Heav'n, Hell, Earth, Chaos, All; the Argument
Held me a while misdoubting his Intent,
That he would ruine (for I saw him strong)
The sacred Truths to Fable and old Song,
(So *Sampson* groap'd the Temples Posts in spight)
10   The World o'rewhelming to revenge his Sight.
    Yet as I read, soon growing less severe,
I lik'd his Project, the success did fear;
Through that wide Field how he his way should find
O're which lame Faith leads Understanding blind;
15   Lest he perplext the things he would explain,
And what was easie he should render vain.
    Or if a Work so infinite he spann'd,
Jealous I was that some less skilful hand
(Such as disquiet always what is well,
20   And by ill imitating would excell)
Might hence presume the whole Creations day
To change in Scenes, and show it in a Play.
    Pardon me, *mighty Poet,* nor despise
My causeless, yet not impious, surmise.
25   But I am now convinc'd, and none will dare
Within thy Labours to pretend a Share.
Thou hast not miss'd one thought that could be fit,
And all that was improper dost omit:
So that no room is here for Writers left,
30   But to detect their Ignorance or Theft.

That Majesty which through thy Work doth Reign
Draws the Devout, deterring the Profane.
And things divine thou treatst of in such state
As them preserves, and Thee inviolate.
35 At once delight and horrour on us seize,
Thou singst with so much gravity and ease;
And above humane flight dost soar aloft,
With Plume so strong, so equal, and so soft.
The *Bird* nam'd from that *Paradise* you sing
40 So never Flags, but alwaies keeps on Wing.
     Where couldst thou Words of such a compass find?
Whence furnish such a vast expense of Mind?
Just Heav'n Thee, like *Tiresias,* to requite,
Rewards with *Prophesie* thy loss of Sight.
45 Well mightst thou scorn thy Readers to allure
With tinkling Rhime, of thy own Sense secure;
While the *Town-Bays* writes all the while and spells,
And like a Pack-Horse tires without his Bells.
Their Fancies like our bushy Points appear,
50 The Poets tag them; we for fashion wear.
I too transported by the *Mode* offend,
And while I meant to *Praise* thee, must Commend.
Thy verse created like thy *Theme* sublime,
In Number, Weight, and Measure, needs not *Rhime.*

HENRY VAUGHAN (1621–1695)

The Night

The Anglo-Welsh devotional poet Vaughan was the twin brother of the occult philosopher Thomas Vaughan, through whom esoteric, Hermetic doctrines filtered into Henry's poems. The twins studied at Jesus College, Oxford, and afterward Henry fought with the Royalists against Cromwell. Later, he became a medical practitioner.

As a poet, Vaughan follows George Herbert and did all his best work from 1650 to 1655. *The Night* weaves its biblical allusions into a remarkably singular texture, centered in John 3:2, where Nicodemus "came to Jesus by night, and said unto him, Rabbi, we know that thou art a teacher from God."

"That sacred veil" is the flesh of Jesus, while "His knocking time" refers to a magnificent verse of Solomon's Song of Songs:

I sleep, but my heart waketh: it is the voice of my beloved that knocketh, saying, Open to me my sister, my love, my dove, my undefiled: for my head is filled with dew and my locks with the drops of the night.

—*Song of Solomon 5:2*

The poem's extraordinary final stanza is Neoplatonic and Hermetic. It posits a Godhead so blazingly dark that he makes all our ordinary perceptions inadequate in comparison.

The Night

JOHN 3:2.

      Through that pure virgin shrine,
That sacred veil drawn o'er thy glorious noon
That men might look and live as glowworms shine
      And face the moon,*
5   Wise Nicodemus saw such light
      As made him know his God by night.

      Most blest believer he!
Who in that land of darkness and blind eyes
Thy long expected healing wings could see,
10   When thou didst rise,†
      And what can never more be done,
      Did at midnight speak with the sun!

      O who will tell me where
He found thee at that dead and silent hour!
15 What hallowed solitary ground did bear
        So rare a flower,
      Within whose sacred leafs did lie
      The fullness of the Deity?

      No mercy seat‡ of gold,
20 No dead and dusty Cherub, nor carved stone,
But his own living works did my Lord hold

---

*"Thou canst not see my face: for there shall no man see me, and live" (Exodus 33:20). Glowworms shine at night.
† Malachi 4:2: "Unto you that fear my name, shall the Sun of righteousness arise with healing in his wings."
‡The golden cover of the ark of the covenant, throne of the invisible presence of God, beneath the wings of cherubim. In the ark were the two stone tablets of the Mosaic law (1 Kings 8:6–9).

And lodge alone;*
    Where trees and herbs did watch and peep
    And wonder,† while the Jews did sleep.

25   Dear night! This world's defeat;‡
    The stop to busy fools; care's check and curb;
    The day of spirits; my soul's calm retreat
            Which none disturb!
          Christ's progress, and his prayer time;§
30   The hours to which high Heaven doth chime.

          God's silent, searching flight:
    When my Lord's head is filled with dew, and all
    His locks are wet with the clear drops of night;
            His still, soft call;
35   His knocking time; the soul's dumb watch,
          When spirits their fair kindred catch.

          Were all my loud, evil days
    Calm and unhaunted as is thy dark tent,
    Whose peace but by some angel's wing or voice
40   Is seldom rent,
          Then I in Heaven all the long year
          Would keep and never wander here.

          But living where the sun
    Doth all things wake, and where all mix and tire

---

*I.e., his own living work (a human being), and that alone, held and lodged the Lord (not the ark revered by the Jews).
†Cf. "And do they so?" (p. 597), for inanimate creatures awareness of the creator.
‡This stanza and the next are a series of appositions characterizing night.
§In the 1655 edition, Vaughan cites Mark 1:35: "in the morning, rising up a great while before day, he went out, and departed into a solitary place, and there he prayed." *Progress:* region or distance traversed during a state journey.

45 Themselves and others, I consent and run
               To every mire,
            And by this world's ill-guiding light,
            Err more than I can do by night.

               There is in God (some say)*
50 A deep but dazzling darkness, as men here
   Say it is late and dusky because they
               See not all clear;
            O for that night! where I in him
            Might live invisible and dim.

*E.g., Dionysius the Areopagite (also called Pseudo-Dionysius), highly influential among Renais-
sance Neoplatonists. In *Mystical Theology*, he develops the idea of a divine darkness so intense that
it outshines all brilliance.

From *The Secular Masque*

Born to Protestant country gentry, Dryden attended Cambridge University and then worked with John Milton and Andrew Marvell in Cromwell's regime. With the Restoration he began his movement to the Stuart cause and became a successful dramatist. In 1668, he was appointed poet laureate. When James II became king, Dryden converted to Roman Catholicism. Loyal to James, he was to be turned out of his public offices after the Stuart monarchy was deposed.

Dryden died on May Day 1700, as England neared the start of the eighteenth century (then considered to be 1701), when he was to be taken up as a precursor of Alexander Pope's and Jonathan Swift's Augustan age in literature. A subtle and dialectical thinker, Dryden had immense energy and challenging skill, equally supple in prose or in verse.

At the end of his life, Dryden composed *The Secular Masque,* to mark the turn between centuries. I give its boisterous conclusion here. Its verve makes it appropriate for any transition, and I recommend chanting the chorus aloud at every New Year, while drinking a toast in memory of its genial author.

From *The Secular Masque*

[*Enter Janus.*]

Janus.   Chronos, Chronos, mend thy Pace,
An hundred times the rowling Sun
Around the Radiant Belt has run
In his revolving Race.
Behold, behold, the Goal in sight,
Spread thy Fans, and wing thy flight.

* * *

Janus.   Then our Age was in it's Prime,
Chronos.   Free from Rage.
Diana.   And free from Crime.
Momus.   A very Merry, Dancing, Drinking,
Laughing, Quaffing, and unthinking Time.
Chorus of all.   *Then our Age was in it's Prime,*
Free from Rage, and free from Crime,
A very Merry, Dancing, Drinking,
Laughing, Quaffing, and unthinking Time.

* * *

Momus.   All, all, of a piece throughout;
[*Pointing to Diana.*]   Thy Chase had a Beast in View;
[*To Mars.*]   Thy Wars brought nothing about;
[*To Venus.*]   Thy Lovers were all untrue.
Janus.   'Tis well an Old Age is out,
Chronos.   And time to begin a New.
Chorus of all.   *All, all, of a piece throughout;*
Thy Chase had a Beast in View;
Thy Wars brought nothing about;
Thy Lovers were all untrue.
'Tis well an Old Age is out,
And time to begin a New.

JOHN WILMOT, EARL OF ROCHESTER (1647–1680)

Upon Nothing

Rochester, the outstanding rakehell at the libertine court of Charles II, set a standard for a poet's lewdness not to be surpassed before the advent of the all-time champion, Lord Byron.

A disciple of Epicurus and Lucretius, and even more of Thomas Hobbes, Rochester is an impressive poetic apostle of materialism.

Dying at thirty-three, Rochester became pious, received the Christian sacrament, and departed repentant.

Upon Nothing, one of his final poems, is a fitter farewell to the life he lived and emphasizes the satiric element in his metaphysical materialism. Its concluding tercets delight me.

Upon Nothing

Nothing thou Elder Brother even to Shade
Thou hadst a being ere the world was made
And (well fixt) art alone of ending not afraid.

Ere Time and Place were, Time and Place were not
When Primitive Nothing, somthing straight begott
Then all proceeded from the great united what—

Somthing, the Generall Attribute of all
Severed from thee its sole Originall
Into thy boundless selfe must undistinguisht fall.

10   Yet Somthing did thy mighty power command
And from thy fruitfull Emptinesses hand
Snatcht, Men, Beasts, birds, fire, water, Ayre, and land.

Matter, the Wickedst offspring of thy Race
By forme assisted flew from thy Embrace
And Rebell-Light obscured thy Reverend dusky face.

With forme and Matter, Time and Place did joyne
Body thy foe with these did Leagues combine
To spoyle thy Peaceful Realme and Ruine all thy Line.

But Turncote-time assists the foe in vayne
20   And brib'd by thee destroyes their short liv'd Reign
And to thy hungry wombe drives back thy slaves again.

Though Misteries are barr'd from Laick Eyes
And the Divine alone with warrant pries
Into thy Bosome, where thy truth in private lyes

Yet this of thee the wise may truly say
Thou from the virtuous Nothing doest delay
And to be part of thee the wicked wisely pray.

Great Negative how vainly would the wise
Enquire, define, distinguish, teach, devise,
30   Didst Thou not stand to poynt their blind Phylosophies.

Is or is not, the two great Ends of Fate
And true or false the Subject of debate
That pérfect or destroy the vast designes of State—

When they have wrackt the Politicians Brest
Within thy Bosome most Securely rest
And when reduc't to thee are least unsafe and best.

But (Nothing) why does Somthing still permitt
That Sacred Monarchs should at Councell sitt
With persons highly thought, at best for nothing fitt,

40   Whilst weighty Somthing modestly abstaynes
From Princes Coffers and from Statesmens braines
And nothing there like Stately nothing reignes?

Nothing who dwell'st with fooles in grave disguise
For whom they Reverend Shapes and formes devise
Lawn-sleeves and Furrs and Gowns, when they like thee
    looke wise:

French Truth, Dutch Prowess, Brittish policy
Hibernian Learning, Scotch Civility
Spaniards Dispatch, Danes witt, are Mainly seen in thee;

The Great mans Gratitude to his best freind
50   Kings promises, Whores vowes towards thee they bend
Flow Swiftly into thee, and in thee ever end.

JONATHAN SWIFT (1667–1745)

The Day of Judgment

Perhaps the strongest ironist in the world's literature, Swift also may be the outstanding prose stylist of the English language. His masterwork, *A Tale of a Tub,* unfortunately is now read only by scholars and their students, and *Gulliver's Travels,* in truncated form, circulates as a book for children.

Born in Ireland but of English parentage, Swift studied at Trinity College, Dublin. He served as secretary to the diplomat Sir William Temple, joining Temple's household near London.

After Temple's death, Swift returned to Ireland as an Anglican priest. In 1707, the Church sent him to the court of Queen Anne in London, seeking royal funding. During a year in London, Swift befriended the essayist Joseph Addison and was part of the Whig literary circle. Coming back to London in 1710, he joined the Tories and became their spokesman. During the next four years, he associated with Alexander Pope and Pope's literary group.

When the Tory government fell, Swift sadly went to Dublin as dean of St. Patrick's Cathedral. Except for some trips to London, he resigned himself to what he thought a kind of literary exile. In his final years, an ear disorder deranged him and blurred his memories.

Swift was only secondarily a poet, but his sharp, distinctive style nevertheless produced some memorable works. One of these is the late poem *The Day of Judgment,* a nightmare meditation, which avoids impiety by substituting Jove for the Christian god. With characteristic irony, Swift's Jove tells us that our pleasure in damning others will become an instance of the biter bit, as we are dismissed for our malice and foolishness.

The Day of Judgment

With a Whirl of Thought oppress'd,
I sink from Reverie to Rest.
An horrid Vision seiz'd my Head,
I saw the Graves give up their Dead.
Jove, arm'd with Terrors, burst the Skies,
And Thunder roars, and Light'ning flies!
Amaz'd, confus'd, its Fate unknown,
The World stands trembling at his Throne.
While each pale Sinner hangs his Head,
10 Jove, nodding, shook the Heav'ns, and said,
"Offending Race of Human Kind,
By Nature, Reason, Learning, blind;
You who thro' Frailty step'd aside,
And you who never fell—*thro' Pride;*
You who in different Sects have shamm'd,
And come to see each other damn'd;
(So some Folks told you, but they knew
No more of Jove's Designs than you)
The World's mad Business now is o'er,
20 And I resent these Pranks no more.
I to such Blockheads set my Wit!
I damn such Fools!—Go, go, you're bit."

ALEXANDER POPE (1688–1744)

From *The Dunciad* [Book IV]

P ope no longer has an audience among common readers, and this saddens me. As I age I turn to him more frequently because he gives pleasure and insight of a kind both rare and valuable.

Born to Catholic parents, Pope remained loyal to their faith, though he is hardly a Catholic poet. Pope had to battle his fate from adolescence on because his small body was twisted out of shape by tuberculosis. Yet Pope was a prodigy of a poet, and his genius was early recognized. His complete translation of Homer made him wealthy and famous.

Pope became the center of the Tory literary world, closely connected to the government and Queen Anne's court. My favorite among his poems, *The Dunciad,* was published in a three-book version in 1728 and dedicated to Swift. The fourth book, added in 1741, ferociously satirizes the dunces who destroy culture. By then George II, whom Pope abominated, was on the throne and the Tories were out of favor.

In a clear sense, the concluding lines (619 to the end) of *Dunciad* IV constitute Pope's last poem, his apocalypse. I read them and shudder at their relevance: "*Art* after *Art* goes out, and all is Night." Contemplating the replacement of deep reading by cultural studies in the academies, I know what Pope prophesied.

From *The Dunciad* [Book IV]

O Muse! relate (for you can tell alone,
620 Wits have short Memories, and Dunces none)
Relate, who first, who last resign'd to rest;
Whose Heads she partly, whose completely blest;
What Charms could Faction, what Ambition lull,
The Venal quiet, and intrance the Dull;
'Till drown'd was Sense, and Shame, and Right, and Wrong—
O sing, and hush the Nations with thy Song!

* * *

In vain, in vain,—the all-composing Hour
Resistless falls: The Muse obeys the Pow'r.
She comes! she comes! the sable Throne behold
630 Of *Night* Primaeval, and of *Chaos* old!
Before her, *Fancy*'s gilded clouds decay,
And all its varying Rain-bows die away.
Wit shoots in vain its momentary fires,
The meteor drops, and in a flash expires.
As one by one, at dread Medea's strain,
The sick'ning stars fade off th' ethereal plain;
As Argus' eyes by Hermes' wand opprest,
Clos'd one by one to everlasting rest;
Thus at her felt approach, and secret might,
640 *Art* after *Art* goes out, and all is Night.
See skulking *Truth* to her old Cavern fled,
Mountains of Casuistry heap'd o'er her head!
Philosophy, that lean'd on Heav'n before,
Shrinks to her second cause, and is no more.
Physic of *Metaphysic* begs defence,
And *Metaphysic* calls for aid on *Sense!*
See *Mystery* to *Mathematics* fly!

In vain! they gaze, turn giddy, rave, and die.
Religion blushing veils her sacred fires,
650 And unawares *Morality* expires.
Nor *public* Flame, nor *private,* dares to shine;
Nor *human* Spark is left, nor Glimpse *divine!*
Lo! thy dread Empire, CHAOS! is restor'd;
Light dies before thy uncreating word:
Thy hand, great Anarch! lets the curtain fall;
And Universal Darkness buries All.

SAMUEL JOHNSON (1708–1784)

On the Death
of Dr. Robert Levet

Dr. Johnson, in my judgment, remains the canonical literary critic. He was also a superb poet, whose idolatry of Alexander Pope restrained him from developing his own gift. How immensely varied his talents were!

James Boswell's *Life of Johnson* is wonderful in itself and augments our sense of Johnson's human value and achievement. Unfortunately, many read it who never read Johnson, and so never directly encounter a major wisdom writer. A great moralist, like Montaigne and Freud, Johnson resembles them also by not moralizing. His motto is "Clear your mind of cant."

Born a bookseller's son, Johnson studied at Oxford and began as a schoolteacher. At twenty-eight he risked going to London to start a literary career, earning enough to scrape by as a journalist and translator. Fame arrived with his *Dictionary of the English Language,* to be followed by his edition of Shakespeare, three series of essays, and *The Lives of the Poets.* Gathered around Johnson was a group including the actor David Garrick, the orator and writer Edmund Burke, the painter Sir Joshua Reynolds, the dramatist-novelist Oliver Goldsmith, and others. A great conversationalist, Johnson inspired and entertained them, as he does his readers, and Boswell's.

A devout Christian, Johnson nevertheless was obsessed with mortality. This emerges movingly in his essays and poems. Two years before his own death, he wrote a touching elegy, included here, on the death of his friend Robert Levet.

Levet had no medical degree but practiced medicine rather effectively, healing the poor as best he could, for either very small fees or none at all. A silent, gentle man, he lived as part of Johnson's household and is now remembered by this poem.

"Officious" has reversed its meaning over the last two centuries. In the second stanza it means full of good offices.

On the Death of Dr. Robert Levet

Condemn'd to hope's delusive mine,
  As on we toil from day to day,
By sudden blasts, or slow decline,
  Our social comforts drop away.

Well tried through many a varying year,
  See LEVET to the grave descend;
Officious, innocent, sincere,
  Of ev'ry friendless name the friend.

Yet still he fills affection's eye,
10 Obscurely wise, and coarsely kind;
Nor, letter'd arrogance, deny
  Thy praise to merit unrefin'd.

When fainting nature call'd for aid,
  And hov'ring death prepar'd the blow,
His vig'rous remedy display'd
  The power of art without the show.

In misery's darkest caverns known,
  His useful care was ever nigh,
Where hopeless anguish pour'd his groan,
20 And lonely want retir'd to die.

No summons mock'd by chill delay,
  No petty gain disdain'd by pride,
The modest wants of ev'ry day
  The toil of ev'ry day supplied.

His virtues walk'd their narrow round,
   Nor made a pause, nor left a void;
And sure th' Eternal Master found
   The single talent well employ'd.

The busy day, the peaceful night,
   Unfelt, uncounted, glided by;
His frame was firm, his powers were bright,
   Tho' now his eightieth year was nigh.

Then with no throbbing fiery pain,
   No cold gradations of decay,
Death broke at once the vital chain,
   And free'd his soul the nearest way.

WILLIAM COWPER (1731–1800)

The Cast-Away

Cowper (pronounced "Cooper") began as a lawyer, but he found the law too stressful and suffered a depressive breakdown and tried to kill himself. While in an asylum he was converted to Evangelism.

In rural retirement, Cowper composed *The Task,* a valuable long poem once widely read but now neglected. Cowper survives as a poet primarily by *The Cast-Away,* written during the last year of his life. In the *Narrative* of George Anson, an admiral of the British fleet during the Spanish wars, we are told of a sailor swept overboard in the Atlantic while Anson's ship is battling a storm. With great tact, Cowper postpones the parallel between the drowned sailor and the alienated poet until the last stanza, when it comes upon us with dismaying power.

The Cast-Away

Obscurest night involved the sky,
    Th' Atlantic billows roar'd,
When such a destin'd wretch as I
    Wash'd headlong from on board
Of friends, of hope, of all bereft,
His floating home for ever left.

No braver Chief could Albion boast
    Than He with whom he went,
Nor ever ship left Albion's coast
10   With warmer wishes sent,
He loved them both, but both in vain,
Nor Him beheld, nor Her again.

Not long beneath the whelming brine
    Expert to swim, he lay,
Nor soon he felt his strength decline
    Or courage die away;
But waged with Death a lasting strife
Supported by despair of life.

He shouted, nor his friends had fail'd
20   To check the vessels' course,
But so the furious blast prevail'd
    That, pitiless perforce,
They left their outcast mate behind,
And scudded still before the wind.

Some succour yet they could afford,
    And, such as storms allow,

The cask, the coop, the floated cord
   Delay'd not to bestow;
But He, they knew, nor ship nor shore,
30 Whate'er they gave, should visit more.

Nor, cruel as it seem'd, could He
   Their haste, himself, condemn,
Aware that flight in such a sea
   Alone could rescue *them;*
Yet bitter felt it still to die
Deserted, and his friends so nigh.

He long survives who lives an hour
   In ocean, self-upheld,
And so long he with unspent pow'r
40   His destiny repell'd,
And ever, as the minutes flew,
Entreated help, or cried, Adieu!

At length, his transient respite past,
   His comrades, who before
Had heard his voice in ev'ry blast,
   Could catch the sound no more;
For then, by toil subdued, he drank
The stifling wave, and then he sank.

No poet wept him, but the page
50   Of narrative sincere
That tells his name, his worth, his age,
   Is wet with Anson's tear,
And tears by bards or heroes shed
Alike immortalize the Dead.
I, therefore, purpose not or dream,

Descanting on his fate,
  To give the melancholy theme
    A more enduring date,
  But Mis'ry still delights to trace
60 Its semblance in another's case.

No voice divine the storm allay'd,
    No light propitious shone,
When, snatch'd from all effectual aid,
    We perish'd, each, alone;
But I, beneath a rougher sea,
And whelm'd in deeper gulphs than he.

To the Accuser Who Is the God of This World

Blake, prophet and visionary, was one of the most original poets in the language, and is both direct and open in his appeal yet difficult in his mythmaking drive to free women and men from tyranny, whether social, political, religious, or natural bondage. That final fettering is least understood by his readers and is exemplified by the pithy last poem I have chosen. Written in 1818, nine years before his death, it clearly intends to be a final motto we can stand by, since Blake's confidence in his message is beautifully clear with every phrase.

The prophetic poet was born in London to a working-class family and was wholly self-educated. Apprenticed to an engraver, he pursued the craft and art of engraving throughout an intense life, sometimes marked by poverty and societal oppression. In 1782, he married Catherine Boucher, also of a working-class background. The marriage was childless and had some travails but became serene and mutually supportive.

During his lifetime, if he had any public notice, it was as a failed, eccentric painter. But Samuel Taylor Coleridge valued his lyric poems, and artists like Johann Heinrich Fuseli and John Flaxman admired his paintings. In his isolation, he composed and engraved an astonishing series of visionary poems, culminating in the brief epics, *Milton* and *Jerusalem,* which remain endless to meditation and to opening up the reader's own buried capacity for imaginative self-liberation.

Profoundly influenced by the Bible and by the works of John Milton, Blake worked out his own esoteric interpretations of those texts. Though scholarship delights in linking him to arcane traditions, Blake was cheerfully self-reliant and thought through everything for himself. In my judgment, only William Shakespeare and Emily Dickinson, among the poets, were as conceptually independent and powerful as Blake, who held to the Inner Light tradition of radical Protestantism.

In 1793, Blake had engraved a little emblem book, *The Gates of Paradise,* and he reissued it with a new text in 1818, including the epilogue, *To the Accuser Who Is the God of This World.* Satan is the accuser of sin in the book of Job. Blake sees him as the God worshipped by the names of Jesus and Jehovah in our world. Nothing could be more blistering and total as an indictment of societal religion, particularly since it is made not by a skeptic but by a prophet of the True God, the awakened human Imagination. With formidable cheer, Blake tells "my Satan" he is a dunce who cannot see the authentic shape of the human. Even Satan's spouse, the established Church, will be redeemed of its harlotry, and "Kate," Blake's wholesome wife, cannot be transmuted into "Nan," an emblem of British whoredom. The Night of history and nature wanes, and the fallen morning star, Lucifer, is seen as a delusion, haunting but ending, "the lost Travellers Dream under the Hill."

From *The Gates of Paradise*

[Epilogue]

> To The Accuser who is
> The God of This World

Truly My Satan thou art but a Dunce
And dost not know the Garment from the Man
Every Harlot was a Virgin once
Nor canst thou ever change Kate into Nan

Tho thou art Worshipd by the Names Divine
Of Jesus & Jehovah: thou art still
The Son of Morn in weary Nights decline
10 The lost Travellers Dream under the Hill

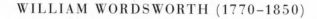

WILLIAM WORDSWORTH (1770–1850)

Extempore Effusion upon the Death of James Hogg

Wordsworth, the inventor of modern poetry, was raised in the Lake District of the north of England. He, his sister, Dorothy, always to be his closest companion, and their three brothers were orphaned very early.

After attending Cambridge University, Wordsworth sojourned in revolutionary France, where he supported the moderate faction who lost out to the Jacobins. He fathered a daughter upon an intrepid reformer, Annette Vallon, but abandoned both of them at the end of 1792, fleeing back to England and five years of deserved remorse. He came out of this crisis by the emotional support of his sister, Dorothy, and the intellectual stimulus of Samuel Taylor Coleridge, who from 1795 became his best friend.

In 1798, Wordsworth and Coleridge published *Lyrical Ballads,* and modern poetry began. The book contained Coleridge's *The Rime of the Ancient Mariner* and Wordsworth's *Tintern Abbey,* both of them poems endlessly influential down to our present time.

The growing inner self is the theme and resource of *Lyrical Ballads.* From Luther to Rousseau this self had burgeoned, but I suspect that Shakespeare was its truest source for Wordsworth and all subsequent poets. Self-consciousness is at once Romanticism's glory and its demon to be exorcised, the work of exorcism being the quest of Wordsworth's strongest poetry.

Wordsworth's best poems all were written in one decade, 1797 to 1807. Forty-three years of mediocrity followed, with just a handful of marvelous exceptions. One of these, his last poem of value, is the *Extempore Effusion,* composed in 1835. It begins as an elegy for the Scottish poet James Hogg, but then becomes a lament for all the makers of his generation recently dead, most notably Coleridge, but also Sir Walter Scott (the Border minstrel), Charles Lamb, George Crabbe, and the rather minor Mrs. Felicia Hemans, the "Her" of the penultimate stanza.

The *Effusion* is most memorable in lamenting the "rapt" and "marvellous" Coleridge, with whom Wordsworth's name and work forever are linked.

Extempore Effusion upon the Death of James Hogg[*]

When first, descending from the moorlands,
I saw the Stream of Yarrow[†] glide
Along a bare and open valley,
The Ettrick Shepherd was my guide.

When last along its banks I wandered,
Through groves that had begun to shed
Their golden leaves upon the pathways,
My steps the Border-minstrel[‡] led.

The mighty Minstrel breathes no longer,
10   'Mid mouldering ruins low he lies;
And death upon the braes[§] of Yarrow,
Has closed the Shepherd-poet's eyes:

Nor has the rolling year twice measured,
From sign to sign, its stedfast course,
Since every mortal power of Coleridge
Was frozen at its marvellous source;

The rapt One, of the godlike forehead,
The heaven-eyed creature sleeps in earth:[¶]

[*]James Hogg: Scottish poet known as "the Ettrick Shepherd," died November 21, 1835.
[†]river in southern Scotland
[‡]Sir Walter Scott had died in 1832.
[§]hillsides
[¶]Coleridge had died in 1834; the two men had been reconciled, but Wordsworth waited a year before elegizing his closest friend, as he so movingly does here.

And Lamb, the frolic and the gentle,
20   Has vanished from his lonely hearth.*

Like clouds that rake the mountain-summits,
Or waves that own no curbing hand,
How fast has brother followed brother,
From sunshine to the sunless land!

Yet I, whose lids from infant slumber
Were earlier raised, remain to hear
A timid voice, that asks in whispers,
"Who next will drop and disappear?"

Our haughty life is crowned with darkness,
30   Like London with its own black wreath,
On which with thee, O Crabbe!† forth-looking.
I gazed from Hampstead's breezy heath.

As if but yesterday departed,
Thou too art gone before; but why,
O'er ripe fruit, seasonably gathered,
Should frail survivors heave a sigh?

Mourn rather for that holy Spirit,
Sweet as the spring, as ocean deep;
For Her‡ who, ere her summer faded,
40   Has sunk into a breathless sleep.

---

*Charles Lamb also had died in 1834.
†George Crabbe had died in 1832.
‡Felicia Hemans, a rather unfortunate poetess, who died at the age of forty-two in 1835; she was very popular for many decades afterward, in America and in England, but is now remembered only for the splendidly bad lyric "Casabianca," with its memorable first line: "The boy stood on the burning deck."

No more of old romantic sorrows,
For slaughtered Youth or love-lorn Maid!
With sharper grief is Yarrow smitten,
And Ettrick mourns with her their Poet dead.

Epitaph

The youngest of the fourteen children of a rural clergyman, Coleridge was a dreamer, and so a very different kind of a person from the start. His adoring father died when he was nine, and Coleridge was sent to school at Christ's Hospital, London, where his close friend was Charles Lamb, who was to become as great an essayist as Coleridge was to mature into a unique poet and major critic.

At Jesus College, Cambridge, Coleridge was unhappy. After a farcical interlude in the British cavalry (the poet kept falling off his horse), he returned to Cambridge but then left without a degree.

With his customary genius for mishap, Coleridge married unhappily. He separated from his wife after a dozen years, being hopelessly in love with Sara Hutchinson, whose sister Mary became Wordsworth's wife. In his dejection, Coleridge became addicted to opium, and from 1816 on, lived in the home of a physician, James Gillman, who helped the poet avoid total collapse.

Gradually Coleridge's poetry ceased, but he did important work as a critic and lay theologian. A year before his death he wrote his last poem in *Epitaph*, intended not for his own memorial tablet but as the final page for an edition of his poetry. In eight lines of gentle pathos, he sums up his life and career, going back to his *Rime of the Ancient Mariner* for the crucial, immensely sad phrase, "death in life."

Epitaph*

Stop, Christian passer-by!—Stop, child of God,
And read with gentle breast. Beneath this sod
A poet lies, or that which once seemed he.
O, lift one thought in prayer for S.T.C.;
That he who many a year with toil of breath
Found death in life, may here find life in death!
Mercy for praise—to be forgiven for† fame
He asked, and hoped, through Christ. Do thou the same!

*not actually written for his own memorial stone, but intended for the final page of an edition of his poems
†instead of

WALTER SAVAGE LANDOR (1775–1864)

Memory

An extraordinary personality, boisterous and quarrelsome, Landor wrote poetry and prose that paradoxically are marked by classical restraint and self-discipline. Yet he had a gift for friendship and was close to Wordsworth and later to Charles Dickens. A wonderful self-deceiver, he idealized himself in *On His Seventy-fifth Birthday:*

> I strove with none, for none was worth my strife:
> Nature I loved, and next to Nature, Art:
> I warmed both hands before the fire of Life:
> It sinks; and I am ready to depart.

In fact, he died in Italy fifteen years later, still keeping up an infinite series of quarrels and lawsuits with his parents, wife, children, friends, and strangers. A year before his death he published his last poem, *Memory,* one of the permanent reflections of old age. At seventy-nine, a decade younger than Landor in this poem, I read it with dark recognition.

Memory

The Mother of the Muses, we are taught,
Is Memory: she has left me; they remain,
And shake my shoulder, urging me to sing
About the summer days, my loves of old.
Alas! alas! is all I can reply.
Memory has left with me that name alone,
Harmonious name, which other bards may sing,
But her bright image in my darkest hour
Comes back, in vain comes back, called or uncalled.
10 Forgotten are the names of visitors
Ready to press my hand but yesterday;
Forgotten are the names of earlier friends
Whose genial converse and glad countenance
Are fresh as ever to mine ear and eye;
To these, when I have written and besought
Remembrance of me, the word *Dear* alone
Hangs on the upper verge, and waits in vain.
A blessing wert thou, O oblivion,
If thy stream carried only weeds away,
20 But vernal and autumnal flowers alike
It hurries down to wither on the strand.

GEORGE GORDON, LORD BYRON (1788–1824)

On This Day I Complete My Thirty-sixth Year

No celebrity, from Cleopatra of Egypt on to our rock super-stars, possibly can compete with Byron, archetype of noto-riety, scandal, and erotic variety—all of them mixed together in a polymorphously perverse brew and then distilled into superb poetry. Byron's epic, *Don Juan,* was judged by Percy Bysshe Shelley to be the poem of the Romantic Age, which Byron loathed, his literary judgment preferring the Augustans, Alexander Pope and Jona-than Swift.

Descended on his mother's side from the Scottish royal family, Byron inherited wealth, rank, and considerable craziness. He was raised by a highly neurotic mother and a sadistic governess. Both at Harrow and at Trinity College, Cambridge, he had homosexual and sadomasoch-istic experience, and then he departed on a grand tour to the Levant and Greece, where his debaucheries were eclectic and manifold. In 1812, he published the first two cantos of *Childe Harold's Pilgrimage,* his travel diary in Spenserian stanzas. Immediately he became the rage of Re-gency London, seduced by scores of noblewomen, while continuing his deepest, incestuous relationship with his half sister. Incredibly hand-some though half lame, a famous athlete and major poet, he became the hero of the Whig aristocracy, on whose behalf he spoke in the House of Lords.

Byron's relationship with Lady Oxford sustained him, but he met his erotic Waterloo in the wild Lady Caroline Lamb, whose husband was to be one of Queen Victoria's prime ministers. Lady Caroline so terrorized Byron that he made the dreadful mistake of marrying an heiress, Annabella Milbank. A disaster from the start, despite the birth of a daughter, the marriage lasted barely a year, since it featured Byron's periodic rages, open and continued incest with his half sister, and his insistence on sodomizing and brutalizing his wife. The separation was a scandal, and Whiggish London ostracized Byron. He exiled himself in 1816, and went to Geneva to begin his close friendship with Shelley, which continued in Italy from 1817 to 1822, when he departed for Greece to lead the rebellion against the Turks. Most of the writing of *Don Juan* belongs to his Italian period, but at thirty-five he was worn out and ready for a heroic death. A year later, he died in Greece of what seems to have been malaria.

His last poem, given below, was written upon his turning thirty-six, three months before dying. Comparing himself, rather dramatically, to William Shakespeare's Macbeth, he remembers his own descent from Banquo, ancestor of the Stuart kings. They are "*whom* / Thy life-blood tracks its parent lake," and he desires a soldier's death in battle, to be worthy of them. Erotic self-aversion is felt throughout the poem, since the noble lord was in love, for a final time, with his Greek page boy Loukas, who refused Byron's advances.

On This Day I Complete My Thirty-sixth Year

'Tis time this heart should be unmoved,*
    Since others it hath ceased to move:
Yet, though I cannot be beloved,
        Still let me love!

My days are in the yellow leaf;†
    The flowers and fruits of love are gone;
The worm, the canker, and the grief
        Are mine alone!

The fire that on my bosom preys
10   Is lone as some volcanic isle;
No torch is kindled at its blaze—
        A funeral pile.

The hope, the fear, the jealous care,
    The exalted portion of the pain
And power of love, I cannot share,
        But wear the chain.

But 'tis not *thus*—and 'tis not *here*—
    Such thoughts should shake my soul, nor *now*,
Where glory decks the hero's bier,
20   Or binds his brow.

The sword, the banner, and the field,
    Glory and Greece, around me see!

*See the last line of *Stanzas to the Po*.
†See Shakespeare's Sonnet LXXIII and *Macbeth* V.III.21 ff.

The Spartan, borne upon his shield,[*]
    Was not more free.

Awake! (not Greece—she *is* awake!)
    Awake, my spirit! Think through *whom*[†]
Thy life-blood tracks its parent lake,
    And then strike home!

Tread those reviving passions down,
30   Unworthy manhood!—unto thee
Indifferent should the smile or frown
    Of beauty be.

If thou regret'st thy youth, *why live?*
    The land of honourable death
Is here:—up to the field, and give
    Away thy breath!

Seek out—less often sought than found—
    A soldier's grave, for thee the best;
Then look around, and choose thy ground,
40   And take thy rest.

[*]Wounded or dead Spartans were honored by being so carried off the battlefield.
[†]Byron was descended (through his mother) from the ancient kings of Scotland.

PERCY BYSSHE SHELLEY (1792–1822)

From *The Triumph of Life*

S helley—together with William Blake, Walt Whitman, Hart Crane, William Shakespeare, John Milton, W. B. Yeats, and Wallace Stevens—is one of the poets I have loved all my life, since I was a child of ten. Born on August 4, 1792, to a wealthy family of rural squires, Shelley was a radical rebel in politics, religion, and literature from his boyhood until his early death at twenty-nine.

After fighting against the system at Eton, Shelley was expelled from Oxford, after only half a year, for publishing a pamphlet, *The Necessity of Atheism*. In London he joined radical circles, and at nineteen eloped with the sixteen-year-old Harriet Westbrook. Despite having had two children with her, Shelley abandoned Harriet for Mary Godwin, the seventeen-year-old daughter of the philosopher reformer William Godwin and the heroic feminist Mary Wollstonecraft, who had died giving birth to the younger Mary. (Mary Godwin Shelley would become the author of *Frankenstein* and of *The Last Man*.) In May 1816, the Shelleys went to Geneva to meet Byron. Back in England, Shelley confronted Harriet's suicide by drowning and was denied custody of their two children by the Lord Chancellor, on moral grounds. In March 1818, Shelley went to Italy in voluntary, permanent exile.

In his four remaining years, Shelley created an extraordinary wealth of lyrical poetry, yet was afflicted by an increasing despair about the human predicament. When he drowned, a month before turning thirty, he left unfinished his greatest poem, *The Triumph of Life*. I give here an excerpt, lines 179 to 247, from Shelley's last poem, which is a Dantesque vision of judgment: this fragment centers on Rousseau, who is Virgil to Shelley's Dante, and so the English visionary's guide to the Inferno of this life. Why Rousseau? Shelley identified with him and gives him the preference over Wordsworth as heroic but self-defeated precursor.

From *The Triumph of Life*

I would have added—"is all here amiss?"

But a voice answered .. "Life" . . . I turned & knew

(O Heaven have mercy on such wretchedness!)

That what I thought was an old root which grew

To strange distortion out of the hill side

Was indeed one of that deluded crew,

And that the grass which methought hung so wide

And white, was but his thin discoloured hair,

And that the holes it vainly sought to hide

Were or had been eyes.*—"If thou canst forbear

To join the dance, which I had well forborne."

190 Said the grim Feature,† of my thought aware,

"I will now tell that which to this deep scorn

Led me & my companions, and relate

The progress of the pageant since the morn;

"If thirst of knowledge doth not thus abate,

Follow it even to the night, but I

Am weary" . . . Then like one who with the weight

Of his own words is staggered, wearily

He paused, and ere he could resume, I cried,

"First who art thou?" . . . "Before thy memory

---

*Rousseau, a great poet (in Shelley's judgment) and thus one of "heaven's living eyes," is fearfully ashamed of his loss, which parallels the blindfolding of the charioteer.

†See *Paradise Lost* X.279; "Feature" used in the sense of form or shape.

200   "I feared, loved, hated, suffered, did, & died,
     And if the spark with which Heaven lit my spirit
       Earth had with purer nutriment supplied

     "Corruption would not now thus much inherit
       Of what was once Rousseau—nor this disguise
    Stained that within which still disdains to wear it.*—

     "If I have been extinguished, yet there rise
    A thousand beacons from the spark I bore."†—
       "And who are those chained to the car?" "The Wise,

     "The great, the unforgotten: they who wore
210   Mitres & helms & crowns, or wreathes of light,‡
    Signs of thought's empire over thought; their lore

     "Taught them not this—to know themselves; their might
    Could not repress the mutiny within,§
       And for the morn of truth they feigned, deep night

     "Caught them ere evening." "Who is he with chin
       Upon his breast and hands crost on his chain?"
    "The Child of a fierce hour; he sought to win

     "The world, and lost all it did contain
    Of greatness, in its hope destroyed; & more
220   Of fame & peace than Virtue's self can gain

---

*The disdain is like that of Farinata (*Inferno* X.36) and the other heroic damned in Dante.
†as one of the founders of Romanticism
‡The saints too are chained to the chariot.
§the unregenerate selfhood

"Without the opportunity which bore
    Him on its eagle's pinion to the peak
From which a thousand climbers have before

"Fall'n as Napoleon fell."—I felt my cheek
Alter to see the great form pass away
    Whose grasp had left the giant world so weak

That every pigmy kicked it as it lay—
    And much I grieved to think how power & will
In opposition rule our mortal day—

230   And why God made irreconcilable
Good & the means of good,* and for despair
    I half disdained mine eye's desire to fill

With the spent vision of the times that were
    And scarce have ceased to be . . . "Dost thou behold,"
Said then my guide, "those spoilers spoiled, Voltaire,

"Frederic, & Kant, Catherine, & Leopold,†
Chained hoary anarchs, demagogue & sage
    Whose name the fresh world thinks already old—

"For in the battle Life & they did wage
240   She remained conqueror—I was overcome
By my own heart alone, which neither age

*Shelley's central and most sorrowful insight
†The "enlightened despots" were Frederick the Great of Prussia, Catherine the Great of Russia, and
Leopold II of Austria, together with Voltaire, the Enlightenment man of letters, who inspired them
to "reforms," and Immanuel Kant, culminating philosopher of the Enlightenment. These make an
odd company, but in the view of the emotional naturalist Rousseau they all neglected the heart and
its impulses.

"Nor tears nor infamy nor now the tomb
Could temper to its object."*—"Let them pass"—
I cried—"the world & its mysterious doom

"Is not so much more glorious than it was
That I desire to worship those who drew
247 New figures on its false & fragile glass

---

*The Enlightened fell victim to life; Rousseau fell victim too, but to his heart's infinite desires, which could not temper themselves to any attainable objects.

JOHN KEATS (1795–1821)

This Living Hand

orn in London on October 31, 1795, Keats was to die in Rome on February 23, 1821, only twenty-five years and four months old. He suffered from hereditary tuberculosis, which had stunted his height to exactly five feet, though nevertheless he was handsome, lively, and pugnacious.

Keats studied medicine but never practiced it. In one wonderful year, from autumn 1818 to autumn 1819, he composed almost all his major poems: the six great odes, many sonnets, the two *Hyperion* fragments, *The Eve of St. Agnes, Lamia,* and crucial lyrics.

From December 1818 on, Keats was in love with Fanny Brawne, but his desperate ill health prevented fulfillment. In the last year of his life, he despaired and wrote almost nothing. His last poem, the fragment *This Living Hand,* probably was written in January 1820. It appears to have been intended for a verse drama never completed.

This Living Hand

This living hand, now warm and capable
Of earnest grasping, would, if it were cold
And in the icy silence of the tomb,
So haunt thy days and chill thy dreaming nights
That thou wouldst wish thine own heart dry of blood
So in my veins red life might stream again,
And thou be conscience-calmed—see here it is—
I hold it towards you.

RALPH WALDO EMERSON (1803–1882)

Terminus

M ore than any other person in the intellectual and literary history of the United States, Emerson was and remains our central mind. Our poets in particular tend to be either in his traditions (there are more than one) or in counter-currents set up against him. And yet his poetry, though splendid at its best, is secondary to his prose: essays, lectures, sermons, but above all his vast journals, his true masterworks.

Born on May 25, 1803, in Boston, he came from a long line of ministers, initially Calvinist and then Unitarian. The family was cursed by tuberculosis, but Emerson himself weathered it, though the disease cost him his beloved first wife, his closest brother, and his firstborn son.

After Harvard and its Divinity School, Emerson served as a Unitarian minister until 1832, when he resigned, went abroad, and returned to take up a freelance career as a secular lecturer and writer. His second marriage sustained him, and he achieved fame and influence through his work.

Fiercely antislavery, Emerson defended John Brown, broke with Daniel Webster on the Fugitive Slave Law, and supported Lincoln. By 1875, Emerson showed signs of what is now known as Alzheimer's disease, and his final seven years were a sorrow.

In the age of Emerson, his many disciples included Walt Whitman, Henry David Thoreau, Margaret Fuller, and the senior Henry James. Edgar Allan Poe, Herman Melville, and Nathaniel Hawthorne defined themselves by dissent from Emerson, yet Captain Ahab and Hester Prynne are Emersonians, as is the Isabel Archer of Henry James. Emily Dickinson kept her distance from the Sage of Concord, but the few poems she published anonymously in her lifetime always were taken to be his.

At sixty-four, Emerson published his eloquent, strong, yet somber last poem, *Terminus*. Accepting limits, it nevertheless insists on riding out "the storm of time."

Terminus

It is time to be old,
To take in sail:—
The god of bounds,
Who sets to seas a shore,
Came to me in his fatal rounds,
And said: "No more!
No farther spread
Thy broad ambitious branches, and thy root.
Fancy departs: no more invent,
10   Contract thy firmament
To compass of a tent.
There's not enough for this and that,
Make thy option which of two;
Economize the failing river,
Not the less revere the Giver,
Leave the many and hold the few.
Timely wise accept the terms,
Soften the fall with wary foot;
A little while
20   Still plan and smile,
And, fault of novel germs,
Mature the unfallen fruit.
Curse, if thou wilt, thy sires,
Bad husbands of their fires,
Who, when they gave thee breath,
Failed to bequeath
The needful sinew stark as once,
The Baresark marrow to thy bones,
But left a legacy of ebbing veins,
30   Inconstant heat and nerveless reins,—

Amid the Muses, left thee deaf and dumb,
Amid the gladiators, halt and numb."

As the bird trims her to the gale,
I trim myself to the storm of time,
I man the rudder, reef the sail,
Obey the voice at eve obeyed at prime:
"Lowly faithful, banish fear,
Right onward drive unharmed;
The port, well worth the cruise, is near,
40   And every wave is charmed."

HENRY WADSWORTH LONGFELLOW (1807–1882)

Elegiac Verse

A wonderful lyric poet, once famous and then neglected, Longfellow merits revival and begins to receive it.

Born in Portland, Maine, Longfellow attended Bowdoin College, with Nathaniel Hawthorne as a classmate. After study abroad, he taught at Bowdoin. Unfortunately his first wife died of a miscarriage. Remarried in 1843, he underwent tragedy again. His second wife, mother of their six children, died in 1861, when her dress caught fire. Vainly attempting to save her, Longfellow was seriously burned.

From 1836 on, Longfellow was professor of modern languages at Harvard. His long poems, *Evangeline* and *The Song of Hiawatha,* were very popular. Good as they remain, his complete translation of Dante's *Divine Comedy* is better, and I prefer it to most current versions.

A learned and dexterous poet, Longfellow wrote a remarkable last poem, *Elegiac Verse,* in the final year of his life. Its tonal shifts constantly surprise as hexameters move in an unnerving progression. Verse XII is curiously Nietzschean in its implication that what can be said is already dead in our hearts, and XIII catches a phenomenon I encounter daily at seventy-nine.

Elegiac Verse

I

Peradventure of old, some bard in Ionian Islands,
  Walking alone by the sea, hearing the wash of the waves,
Learned the secret from them of the beautiful verse elegiac,
  Breathing into his song motion and sound of the sea.

For as the wave of the sea, upheaving in long undulations,
  Plunges loud on the sands, pauses, and turns, and retreats,
So the Hexameter, rising and singing, with cadence sonorous,
  Falls; and in refluent rhythm back the Pentameter flows.

II

Not in his youth alone, but in age, may the heart of the poet
10   Bloom into song, as the gorse blossoms in autumn and spring.

III

Not in tenderness wanting, yet rough are the rhymes of our poet;
  Though it be Jacob's voice, Esau's, alas! are the hands.

IV

Let us be grateful to writers for what is left in the inkstand;
  When to leave off is an art only attained by the few.

V

How can the Three be One? you ask me; I answer by asking,
  Hail and snow and rain, are they not three, and yet one?

VI

By the mirage uplifted, the land floats vague in the ether,
    Ships and the shadows of ships hang in the motionless air;
So by the art of the poet our common life is uplifted,
20   So, transfigured, the world floats in a luminous haze.

VII

Like a French poem is Life; being only perfect in structure
    When with the masculine rhymes mingled the feminine are.

VIII

Down from the mountain descends the brooklet, rejoicing in
    freedom;
    Little it dreams of the mill hid in the valley below;
Glad with the joy of existence, the child goes singing and laughing,
    Little dreaming what toils lie in the future concealed.

IX

As the ink from our pen, so flow our thoughts and our feelings
    When we begin to write, however sluggish before.

X

Like the Kingdom of Heaven, the Fountain of Youth is within us;
30   If we seek it elsewhere, old shall we grow in the search.

XI

If you would hit the mark, you must aim a little above it;
    Every arrow that flies feels the attraction of earth.

XII

Wisely the Hebrews admit no Present tense in their language;
    While we are speaking the word, it is already the Past.

XIII

In the twilight of age all things seem strange and phantasmal,
    As between daylight and dark ghost-like the landscape appears.

XIV

Great is the art of beginning, but greater the art is of ending;
    Many a poem is marred by a superfluous verse.

EDWARD FITZGERALD (1809–1883)

From *The Rubaiyát*
of Omar Khayyám

itzgerald's *Rubaiyát* is the most popular poem in the English language. It is also a work of high aesthetic merit and a dark, Epicurean vision of human life, epigrammatic and memorable throughout its one hundred and one quatrains, of which I give the final sixteen here. In 1879, four years before his death, Fitzgerald had revised it again, and this final sequence can be considered his last poem.

A famous, wealthy eccentric, Fitzgerald blundered into a bad marriage that endured for only a year. For comfort, Fitzgerald created his first version of the *Rubaiyát* and published it in 1859 through an antiquarian bookshop. It was soon remaindered and would have disappeared except that Dante Gabriel Rossetti found a copy, which intoxicated him. Rossetti introduced the poem to his Pre-Raphaelite circle of William Morris, George Meredith, and Algernon Charles Swinburne, all of whom recommended it to the public, which took to it immediately.

Fitzgerald had received the material in rough form from a scholar of Persian. Omar Khayyám was an astronomer and not of the first rank of Persian poets. "Rubaiyát" means quatrains in the rhyme scheme *aaba*.

Iranian critics inform me that Fitzgerald's poetic splendor is entirely his own, and not Omar's.

A close friend of Alfred, Lord Tennyson, Fitzgerald ironically juxtaposes his own nihilism to the measured faith of the laureate's *In Memoriam*. In this final sequence of the *Rubaiyát* the poet goes to a Potter's house and listens to the Vessels complain. The Potter clearly represents a creator god and the Vessels ourselves. Wine and its purchased oblivion must be our solace, and in the final quatrain, Sákí, the wine pourer, is urged to turn down an empty glass in memory of the poet.

From *The Rubaiyát of Omar Khayyám*

86

After a momentary silence spake
Some Vessel of a more ungainly Make;
  "They sneer at me for leaning all awry:
What! did the Hand then of the Potter shake?"

87

Whereat some one of the loquacious Lot—
I think a Súfi pipkin—waxing hot—
  "All this of Pot and Potter—Tell me then,
Who is the Potter, pray, and who the Pot?"

88

"Why," said another, "Some there are who tell
10 Of one who threatens he will toss to Hell
  The luckless Pots he marr'd in making—Pish!
He's a Good Fellow, and 'twill all be well."

89

"Well," murmur'd one, "Let whose make or buy,
My Clay with long Oblivion is gone dry:
  But fill me with the old familiar Juice,
Methinks I might recover by and by."

90

So while the Vessels one by one were speaking,
The little Moon look'd in that all were seeking:
  And then they jogg'd each other. "Brother! Brother!
20 Now for the Porter's shoulder-knot a-creaking!"

91

Ah, with the Grape my fading Life provide,
And wash the Body whence the Life has died,
   And lay me, shrouded in the living Leaf,
By some not unfrequented Garden-side.

92

That ev'n my buried Ashes such a snare
Of Vintage shall fling up into the Air
   As not a True-believer passing by
But shall be overtaken unaware.

93

Indeed the Idols I have loved so long
30   Have done my credit in this World much wrong:
   Have drown'd my Glory in a shallow Cup
And sold my Reputation for a Song.

94

Indeed, indeed, Repentance oft before
I swore—but was I sober when I swore?
   And then and then came Spring, and Rose-in-hand
My thread-bare Penitence apieces tore.

95

And much as Wine has play'd the Infidel,
And robb'd me of my Robe of Honour—Well,
   I wonder often what the Vintners buy
40   One half so precious as the stuff they sell.

96

Yet Ah, that Spring should vanish with the Rose!
That Youth's sweet-scented manuscript should close!
    The Nightingale that in the branches sang,
Ah, whence, and whither flown again, who knows!

97

Would but the Desert of the Fountain yield
One glimpse—if dimly, yet indeed, reveal'd,
    To which the fainting Traveller might spring,
As springs the trampled herbage of the field!

98

Would but some wingèd Angel ere too late
50 Arrest the yet unfolded Roll of Fate,
    And make the stern Recorder otherwise
Enregister, or quite obliterate!

99

Ah, Love! could you and I with Him conspire
To grasp this sorry Scheme of Things entire,
    Would not we shatter it to bits—and then
Re-mould it nearer to the Heart's Desire!

100

Yon rising Moon that looks for us again—
How oft hereafter will she wax and wane;
    How oft hereafter rising look for us
60 Through this same Garden—and for *one* in vain!

101
And when like her, oh, Sákí, you shall pass
Among the Guests Star-scatter'd on the Grass.
    And in your joyous errand reach the spot
Where I made One—turn down an empty Glass!

Crossing the Bar

A few days before his death, Tennyson decided that this lyric was to conclude his complete poems. The "bar" is at once a sandbar at the harbor's mouth and also the barrier between life and the unknown. The "bourne" is a boundary or limit, while the Pilot must be metaphysical, since actual pilots leave the ship once the harbor is cleared.

Tennyson, a great verse artist like Alexander Pope or James Merrill, has rightly recovered from his long eclipse. Born in Lincolnshire, where his father was a rector, Tennyson went to Trinity College, Cambridge, and formed a warm friendship with Arthur Henry Hallam. Two early volumes of poetry (1830 and 1832) were championed by Hallam, a brilliant critic, but he died at twenty-two of a brain seizure. Tennyson's grief, which continued throughout his life, motivated his best poetry. *In Memoriam* is an overt elegy for Hallam, but more subtly much of Tennyson's work besides *In Memoriam* mourns Hallam: *Ulysses, Tithonus, Morte d'Arthur,* and most of *Idylls of the King.*

Crossing the Bar is almost too famous, but read closely it carries readers with it, particularly in the beautiful second stanza, which is as magical as Samuel Taylor Coleridge in *The Rime of the Ancient Mariner* or John Keats in *La Belle Dame Sans Merci*. Like all of Tennyson, this last poem needs to be read aloud slowly.

Crossing the Bar

Sunset and evening star,
    And one clear call for me!
And may there be no moaning of the bar,
    When I put out to sea,

But such a tide as moving seems asleep,
    Too full for sound and foam,
When that which drew from out the boundless deep
    Turns again home.

Twilight and evening bell,
10   And after that the dark!
And may there be no sadness of farewell,
    When I embark;

For though from out our bourne* of Time and Place
    The flood may bear me far,
I hope to see my Pilot face to face
    When I have crossed the bar.

*bourne: boundary or limit

ROBERT BROWNING (1812–1889)

Prologue from *Asolando*

solando, Browning's last volume, was published in London on the same day that he died in Venice. The book's title refers to Asolo, the poet's favorite place, a village near Venice. This prologue, perhaps his last poem, goes back half a century to when Browning first saw Asolo. Developing the Wordsworthian theme of a last visionary glory, Browning burns through loss into a last transcendence.

The first two stanzas feature a Wordsworthian speaker who emphasizes loss, while Browning himself speaks the rest of the poem. With the final word, "transcends," we are given the difficulty of defining Browning's God, who has little to do with Christianity.

Browning was born on May 7, 1812, in London, the oldest child of a wealthy banker and his Evangelical wife, who tried to raise the poet in her faith. Self-educated at home in his father's large library, he endured no university, which his fierce will could not have tolerated. At fourteen he became a passionate reader of Percy Bysshe Shelley, an attachment that was to be permanent. His published poetry began with three long Shelleyan quest romances. By a singular act of self-reinvention, he transfigured Shelley's lyricism into the dramatic monologue, his particular innovation in poetic form, though arrived at by Alfred Lord Tennyson independently.

For a remarkable span, January 1845 until September 1846, when they eloped together to Italy, Browning and the poet Elizabeth Barrett corresponded, meeting only rarely. The marriage unfortunately lasted only fifteen years: she died in Florence in June 1861, leaving Browning with an eleven-year-old son. The poet never remarried, made something of a myth of his lost happiness, but became madly sociable in both Italy and England and seems to have found solace with several devoted women.

Browning's great works are the two volumes of dramatic mono-logues, *Men and Women,* and a long poem made up of monologues, *The Ring and the Book.* He is, in my judgment, the greatest and most original poet in English since the High Romantics and Walt Whitman, un-surpassed by the major modern poets: W. B. Yeats, Wallace Stevens, D. H. Lawrence, or Hart Crane. My students find him initially difficult but finally immensely rewarding. He needs deep reading and teaches it.

Prologue from *Asolando*

PROLOGUE

"The Poet's age is sad: for why?
   In youth, the natural world could show
No common object but his eye
   At once involved with alien glow—
His own soul's iris-bow.*

"And now a flower is just a flower:
   Man, bird, beast are but beast, bird, man—
Simply themselves, uncinct† by dower
   Of dyes which, when life's day began,
10 Round each in glory ran."

Friend, did you need an optic glass,
   Which were your choice? A lens to drape
In ruby, emerald, chrysopras,‡
   Each object—or reveal its shape
Clear outlined, past escape,

The naked very thing?—so clear
   That, when you had the chance to gaze,
You found its inmost self appear
   Through outer seeming—truth ablaze,
20 Not falsehood's fancy-haze?

*iris-bow: rainbow
†uncinct: not surrounded
‡chrysopras: apple-green chalcedony, a precious stone

How many a year, my Asolo,
　　Since—one step just from sea to land—
I found you, loved yet feared you so—
　　For natural objects seemed to stand
Palpably fire-clothed! No—

No mastery of mine o'er these!
　　Terror with beauty, like the Bush*
Burning but unconsumed. Bend knees,
　　Drop eyes to earthward! Language? Tush!
30　Silence 'tis awe decrees.

And now? The lambent flame is—where?
　　Lost from the naked world: earth, sky,
Hill, vale, tree, flower,—Italia's rare
　　O'er-running beauty crowds the eye—
But flame? The Bush is bare.

Hill, vale, tree, flower—they stand distinct,
　　Nature to know and name. What then?
A Voice spoke thence which straight unlinked
　　Fancy from fact: see, all's in ken:†
40　Has once my eyelid winked?

No, for the purged ear apprehends
　　Earth's import, not the eye late dazed:
The Voice said "Call my works thy friends!
　　At Nature dost thou shrink amazed?
God is it who transcends."

---

*See Exodus 3:2, the manifestation of Jehovah to Moses in the burning bush.
†knowledge, apprehension, perhaps here sight

Last Lines

t twenty-eight, a year before *Wuthering Heights* was published, Emily Brontë composed what Charlotte Brontë thought were her sister's last lines. Only thirty at her death by tuberculosis, the family malady, Emily was a great if sparse poet, whose single novel remains unique in its kind, surpassing Charlotte's *Jane Eyre,* vital as that continues to be.

Lord Byron, the original of Heathcliff and Rochester, was central to the sisters' personal mythmaking, but I find nothing ironic in Emily Brontë's strongest poems. The noble, narcissistic Lord Byron retained a nostalgia for Christianity, but Emily is proudly, defiantly a Gnostic heretic, despite her clerical father. In *Last Lines,* the "God within my breast" is akin to the ancient Gnostic "spark" or *pneuma,* the best and oldest part of the soul. The poem repudiates all creeds and affirms instead the Stranger God, at once exiled from our world yet present also, buried deep in the self.

Last Lines

No coward soul is mine,
No trembler in the world's storm-troubled sphere;
   I see Heaven's glories shine,
And faith shines equal, arming me from fear.

   O God within my breast,
Almighty, ever-present Deity!
   Life—that in me has rest,
As I—undying Life—have power in Thee!

   Vain are the thousand creeds
10 That move men's hearts—unutterably vain;
   Worthless as withered weeds,
Or idlest froth amid the boundless main,

   To waken doubt in one
Holding so fast by Thine infinity;
   So surely anchored on
The steadfast rock of immortality.

   With wide-embracing love
Thy spirit animates eternal years,
   Pervades and broods above,
20 Changes, sustains, dissolves, creates, and rears.

   Though earth and man were gone,
And suns and universes ceased to be,
   And Thou were left alone,
Every existence would exist in Thee.

There is not room for Death,
Nor atom that his might could render void;
    Thou—Thou art Being and Breath,
And what that Thou art may never be destroyed.

WALT WHITMAN (1819–1892)

Night on the Prairies

The major American poet, matched if at all only by Emily Dickinson, wrote a series of last poems throughout his long career. Two sections of the final *Leaves of Grass* abound in self-elegiac farewells: *Whispers of Heavenly Death* and *Songs of Parting.* I first thought of choosing the marvelous *The Last Invocation* for this gathering, but instead am refreshed more by *Night on the Prairies,* a poem of 1860, when the poet was only forty-one, with thirty-two years still to live.

Whitman's life itself is an American poem, but then he declared that the United States was the greatest poem. An autodidact, like William Blake and Robert Browning, he was the son of Walter Whitman, a dissident Long Island Quaker carpenter, and his wife, Louise. Whitman learned the printer's trade in the offices of Brooklyn newspapers and worked much of his life as a Manhattan journalist. Reading Ralph Waldo Emerson's essays throughout 1854 and 1855, he was kindled into composing the first *Leaves of Grass,* printed and bound by himself and mailed to Emerson, who responded in an extraordinary letter, hailing the book for its unmatched American wit and wisdom.

Though recognition, despite Emerson's encouragement, came slowly,

Whitman was launched. New editions of *Leaves of Grass* came forth in 1856 and 1860, to be followed by *Drum-Taps* in 1865. From 1863 to 1864, the poet served as an unpaid volunteer wound-dresser and nurse in the Civil War hospitals of Washington, DC. His imaginative apotheosis came in 1865 with the composition of *When Lilacs Last in the Dooryard Bloom'd,* his elegy for the martyred Abraham Lincoln, who was to American presidents what Whitman is to American poets: the sublime summit.

Night on the Prairies

Night on the prairies,
The supper is over, the fire on the ground burns low,
The wearied emigrants sleep, wrapt in their blankets;
I walk by myself—I stand and look at the stars, which I think
    now I never realized before.

5   Now I absorb immortality and peace,
I admire death and test propositions.

How plenteous! how spiritual! how resumé!
The same old man and soul—the same old aspirations, and
    the same content.

I was thinking the day most splendid till I saw what the not-
    day exhibited,
10   I was thinking this globe enough till there sprang out so
    noiseless around me myriads of other globes.

Now while the great thoughts of space and eternity fill me I
    will measure myself by them,
And now touch'd with the lives of other globes arrived as far
    along as those of the earth,
Or waiting to arrive, or pass'd on farther than those of the earth,
I henceforth no more ignore them than I ignore my own life.
15   Or the lives of the earth arrived as far as mine, or waiting to
    arrive.

O I see now that life cannot exhibit all to me, as the day cannot,
I see that I am to wait for what will be exhibited by death.

HERMAN MELVILLE (1819–1891)

Shelley's Vision

W hat are the inescapable American literary classics? Only a few have won general agreement, but they include Ralph Waldo Emerson's complete *Journals,* Nathaniel Hawthorne's *The Scarlet Letter,* Henry David Thoreau's *Walden,* Mark Twain's *Adventures of Huckleberry Finn,* Walt Whitman's *Leaves of Grass,* and Melville's *Moby-Dick,* which has eclipsed many other works by Melville, his poetry included.

After he began his career as a writer with *Typee* (1846), which sold very well, Melville never again enjoyed a commercial success. *Moby-Dick* (1851) drew only mild interest, and after that Melville went through many failures and a series of melancholic breakdowns. His marriage to Eleanor Metcalf was endlessly difficult, partly because of his repressed homoeroticism. Perhaps Melville's most intense feeling was for Hawthorne, a good friend but very happy with his wife, Sophia, and his own writing.

In 1867, the Melvilles' oldest son killed himself. In Melville's final years he wrote mostly poetry, including a long poem, *Clarel,* about his pilgrimage to Palestine.

Melville's poetry is rather like Thomas Hardy's but rougher, more abrupt. Like Hardy, he was greatly influenced by Percy Bysshe Shelley, both the poems and the life. Just before Shelley drowned, he met his own image or double while walking in a garden and fainted when the apparition asked him: "How long do you mean to be content?" That seems to have inspired Melville's *Shelley's Vision,* which I have chosen as a last poem because it sums up Melville's own life and work.

Shelley's Vision

Wandering late by morning seas
When my heart with pain was low—
Hate the censor pelted me—
Deject I saw my shadow go.

In elf-caprice of bitter tone
I too would pelt the pelted one:
At my shadow I cast a stone.

When lo, upon that sun-lit ground
I saw the quivering phantom take
10   The likeness of Saint Stephen crowned:
Then did self-reverence awake.

MATTHEW ARNOLD (1822–1888)

Growing Old

I have very mixed emotions and judgments concerning both Arnold's literary criticism and his poems, yet am willing to regard him as one of my blind spots. He enjoys the high esteem of both the late Lionel Trilling and Christopher Ricks, each a fine critic.

The son of the formidable Thomas Arnold, headmaster of Rugby School, the poet-critic attended Balliol College, Oxford, and formed a close friendship with the poet Arthur Hugh Clough. He became an inspector of schools and eventually professor of poetry at Oxford. By 1867, his writing of poetry essentially was over.

I have chosen *Growing Old* from *New Poems* (1867). Though Arnold was only forty-five and had twenty-one years still to live, reading *Growing Old* at seventy-nine, I murmur recognition at Arnold's accuracy yet shake my head at "frozen up within."

Growing Old*

What is it to grow old?
Is it to lose the glory of the form,
The lustre of the eye?
Is it for beauty to forego her wreath?
—Yes, but not this alone.

Is it to feel our strength—
Not our bloom only, but our strength—decay?
Is it to feel each limb
Grow stiffer, every function less exact,
10 Each nerve more loosely strung?

Yes, this, and more; but not
Ah, 'tis not what in youth we dreamed 'twould be!
'Tis not to have our life
Mellowed and softened as with sunset-glow,
A golden day's decline.

'Tis not to see the world
As from a height, with rapt prophetic eyes,
And heart profoundly stirred;
And weep, and feel the fulness of the past,
20 The years that are no more.†

It is to spend long days
And not once feel that we were ever young;

*This seems an ironic reply both to Browning ("Rabbi Ben Ezra") and to Wordsworth's consoling
reflections upon old age.
†an echo, without irony, of Tennyson's "Tears, Idle Tears"

It is to add, immured
In the hot prison of the present, month
To month with weary pain.

It is to suffer this,
And feel but half, and feebly, what we feel.
Deep in our hidden heart
Festers the dull remembrance of a change,
30   But no emotion—none.

It is—last stage of all—
When we are frozen up within, and quite
The phantom of ourselves,
To hear the world applaud the hollow ghost
Which blamed the living man.

A Ballad of Past Meridian

eredith, still appreciated as a novelist, is also one of the indispensable poets, though now neglected. His darkly memorable *A Ballad of Past Meridian* was written when he was fifty-four. He lived another twenty-seven years, but this is his keynote poem, admirably expressive of his final stances toward both death and life.

I urge you, as I do my students, to read Meredith's three major novels: *The Ordeal of Richard Feverel* (1859), *The Egoist* (1879)—a comic masterpiece—and *Diana of the Crossways* (1885).

Another autodidact, Meredith broke in as a literary journalist and married the very lively daughter of Percy Bysshe Shelley's friend Thomas Love Peacock, comic novelist and poet. Nine years of quarrels ended when she mercifully eloped with a painter. The ravaged Meredith recovered by writing the *Modern Love* sequence of sixteen-line quasi-sonnets, while crazily moving in to share a London house with his friends Dante Gabriel Rossetti and Algernon Charles Swinburne. A happy second marriage saved Meredith from this perfectly mad household, overrun by Rossetti's menagerie of exotic animals and by the floods of alcohol and drugs consumed by both poets.

A Ballad of Past Meridian*

Last night returning from my twilight walk
I met the grey mist Death, whose eyeless brow
Was bent on me, and from his hand of chalk
He reached me flowers as from a withered bough.
O Death, what bitter nosegays givest thou!

Death said, "I gather," and pursued his way.
Another stood by me, a shape in stone,
Sword-hacked and iron-stained, with breasts of clay,
And metal veins that sometimes fiery shone.
10   O Life, how naked and how hard when known!

Life said, "As thou hast carved me, such am I."
Then Memory, like the nightjar on the pine,
And sightless Hope, a woodlark in night sky,
Joined notes of Death and Life till night's decline.
Of Death, of Life, those inwound notes are mine.

*Past Meridian: Past the period of a person's greatest elevation (see Wallace Stevens's *Le Monocle de Mon Oncle* II.9: "No spring can follow past meridian," where "meridian" is forty)

DANTE GABRIEL ROSSETTI (1828–1882)

Insomnia

*I*nsomnia may have been the last poem Rossetti wrote, a year before his death. As in his masterpiece, *The Stream's Secret* (1869–1870), where the references fuse his wife, Elizabeth Siddal (who killed herself), and his lover, Jane Burden, wife of William Morris, his closest friend, so *Insomnia* amalgamates them as a single dream figure.

Rossetti, born in London to a refugee scholar from Naples and his half-English wife, thought of himself primarily as a painter. I greatly prefer his poems to his pictures, though their enigmas disturb me. A disciple of John Keats and Dante, Rossetti thinks through his poems more thoroughly than anyone now writing.

How Rossetti, alcoholic and drug-laden, lived to fifty-four is a wonder to me. I strongly recommend the late Ken Russell's short film, *Dante's Inferno,* with the late Oliver Reed playing Rossetti. An insomniac myself, I recite this last poem frequently at about 3 A.M., and recommend it to my fellow sufferers.

Insomnia

Thin are the night-skirts left behind
  By daybreak hours that onward creep,
  And thin, alas! the shred of sleep
That wavers with the spirit's wind:
5 But in half-dreams that shift and roll
  And still remember and forget,
My soul this hour has drawn your soul
    A little nearer yet.

Our lives, most dear, are never near,
10 Our thoughts are never far apart,
  Though all that draws us heart to heart
Seems fainter now and now more clear.
To-night Love claims his full control,
  And with desire and with regret
15 My soul this hour has drawn your soul
    A little nearer yet.

Is there a home where heavy earth
  Melts to bright air that breathes no pain,
  Where water leaves no thirst again
20 And springing fire is Love's new birth?
If faith long bound to one true goal
  May there at length its hope beget,
My soul that hour shall draw your soul
    For ever nearer yet.

CHRISTINA ROSSETTI (1830–1894)

Passing Away

T wo years younger than her brother, Christina Rossetti is a very different but equally powerful poet. She is not of the eminence of Emily Dickinson, born in the same year, but then who is? Like her brother and Dickinson, Rossetti is both an erotic and a devotional poet, though she is far more a normative Christian than the other two.

As an independent and original theologian, she meshed Anglicanism and Adventism. Declining at least two substantive marriage proposals, she remained strongly independent. In 1860, turning thirty, she composed the great lyric *Passing Away,* which I take as her last word, though she lived and wrote for more than a third of a century afterward.

Chant *Passing Away* out loud to yourself while thinking your path through it. Superbly it sustains itself upon a single rhyme, while it weaves together allusions to and variations on the Song of Songs. I cannot praise it more highly than to observe how worthy *Passing Away* is of its Solomonic model.

Passing Away*

Passing away, saith the World, passing away:
Chances, beauty, and youth, sapped day by day:
Thy life never continueth in one stay.
Is the eye waxen dim, is the dark hair changing to grey
That hath won neither laurel nor bay?†
I shall clothe myself in Spring and bud in May:
Thou, root-stricken, shalt not rebuild thy decay
On my bosom for aye.
Then I answered: Yea.

10   Passing away, saith my Soul, passing away:
With its burden of fear and hope, of labour and play,
Hearken what the past doth witness and say:
Rust in thy gold, a moth is in thine array,
A canker is in thy bud, thy leaf must decay.
A midnight, at cockcrow, at morning, one certain day
Lo the Bridegroom shall come and shall not delay;‡
Watch thou and pray.
Then I answered: Yea.

Passing away, saith my God, passing away:
20   Winter passeth§ after the long delay:
New grapes on the vine, new figs on the tender spray,
Turtle calleth turtle in Heaven's May.

*This virtuoso lyric on one rhyme is a farewell to the poetess's twenties, being written on the last day of a decade, and a study toward a farewell to all worldliness.
†At this time she was scarcely recognized as a poet.
‡a beautiful use of Christ's parable of the wise and foolish virgins; see Matthew 25:1-13
§This and most of the stanza closely echo Song of Solomon 2:11-13.

Though I tarry, wait for Me, trust Me, watch and pray:
Arise, come away, night is past and lo it is day,
My love, My sister, My spouse, thou shalt hear Me say.
Then I answered: Yea.

EMILY DICKINSON (1830–1886)

The Saddest Noise

It is accurate to observe that in conceptual scope, originality, and profundity Dickinson surpasses any other literary mind since William Shakespeare's. This makes her both elliptical and richly difficult. You can read and teach her for a lifetime and still find yourself always commencing anew.

The definitive edition, *The Poems of Emily Dickinson,* edited by R. W. Franklin, contains 1,789 poems and fragments, the last hundred undated. Though I hardly assume that poem 1,789 necessarily was her very last, it always reads that way—to me. The insouciance of "all the dead / That sauntered with us here" is the purest Dickinson.

No one has improved on my late friend Richard Sewall's biography of Dickinson, which rids us of any current academic myths that the poet had a sexual relationship with her zany sister-in-law Sue. Her actual erotic interests, in sequence, were the Reverend Charles Wadsworth, Samuel Bowles, and, most important, Judge Otis Lord. Sewall makes clear that after the death of Mrs. Lord, Dickinson and Judge Lord were in a kind of secret marriage. He died in 1887, and she followed two years later.

From childhood on, Dickinson was nonconformist in religion. In our contemporary America, no one would consider her Christian. Dickinson's Jesus was not her redeemer; she did not believe in his or a general Resurrection. He was for her the exemplary sufferer, allied to her hopes for triumphing over her own anguishes, the losses of those she loved.

The Saddest Noise 1789

The saddest noise, the sweetest noise,
The maddest noise that grows,—
The birds, they make it in the spring,
At night's delicious close,

5   Between the March and April line—
That magical frontier
Beyond which summer hesitates,
Almost too heavenly near.

It makes us think of all the dead
10   That sauntered with us here,
By separation's sorcery
Made cruelly more dear.

It makes us think of what we had,
And what we now deplore.
15   We almost wish those siren throats
Would go and sing no more.

An ear can break a human heart
As quickly as a spear.
We wish the ear had not a heart
20   So dangerously near.

From *The Story of Sigurd the Volsung*

Morris can be seen all around us: window designs, tapestries, bookbindings, wallpaper, men's neckties and women's dresses, furniture, ornaments, carpets. That, and his Socialist crusading, sometimes obscures his achievements in lyric and narrative poetry and in prose romance.

His personal life was uneasy. An early attachment to a beloved sister shadowed his marriage to the beautiful and mercurial Jane Burden, whose long, painful love affair with Dante Gabriel Rossetti caused considerable suffering both to the lovers and to the reticent Morris.

I have a great fondness for many long poems of the nineteenth century, including Morris's book-length *Sigurd the Volsung* (1876). Though composed twenty years before his death, it is Morris's last venture into heroic poetry, and its reverberating final cadences intimate his own sense of an ending. His travels in Iceland and his translation of the *Volsunga Saga* flower in his vision of the revenge of Gudrun upon King Atli and her suicide, so as to rejoin her slain husband, Sigurd the Volsung.

Though Morris was influenced by Alfred, Lord Tennyson, his unique directness, total detachment in narrating savage violence, and swiftness in movement are entirely his own. Unlike Tennyson, Morris never intrudes with his own moralizing judgments.

From *The Story of Sigurd the Volsung*

And they deemed that their house was fallen to the innermost place
    of the dead,
The hall for the traitors builded, the house of the changeless plain;
They cried, and their tongues were confounded, and none gave
    answer again:
They rushed, and came nowither; each man beheld his foe,
And smote as the hopeless and dying, nor brother brother might
    know,
The sons of one mother's sorrow in the fire-blast strove and smote,
And the sword of the first-begotten was thrust in the father's throat,
And the father hewed at his stripling; the thrall at the war-king
    cried
And mocked the face of the mighty in that house of Atli's pride.

10   There Gudrun stood o'er the turmoil; there stood the Niblung
    child;
As the battle-horn is dreadful, as the winter wind is wild,
So dread and shrill was her crying and the cry none heeded or
    heard,
As she shook the sword in the Eastland, and spake the hidden
    word:

"The brand for the flesh of the people, and the sword for the king of
    the world!"
Then adown the hall and the smoke-cloud the half-slaked torch she
    hurled
And strode to the chamber of Atli, white-fluttering mid the smoke;
But their eyen met in the doorway and he knew the hand and the
    stroke,

And shrank aback before her; and no hand might he upraise,
There was nought in his heart but anguish in that end of Atli's days.

20   But she towered aloft before him, and cried in Atli's home:
"Lo, lo, the day-light, Atli, and the last foe overcome!"
And with all the might of the Niblungs she thrust him through and
    fled,
And the flame was fleet behind her and hung o'er the face of the
    dead.

There was none to hinder Gudrun, and the fire-blast scathed her
    nought,
For the ways of the Norns she wended, and her feet from the wrack
    they brought
Till free from the bane of the East-folk, the swift pursuing flame,
To the uttermost wall of Atli and the side of the sea she came:
She stood on the edge of the steep, and no child of man was there:
A light wind blew from the sea-flood and its waves were little and
    fair,
30   And gave back no sign of the burning, as in twinkling haste they
    ran,
White-topped in the merry morning, to the walls and the havens of
    man.

Then Gudrun girded her raiment, on the edge of the steep she
    stood,
She looked o'er the shoreless water, and cried out o'er the
    measureless flood.
"O Sea, I stand before thee; and I who was Sigurd's wife!
By his brightness unforgotten I bid thee deliver my life
From the deeds and the longing of days, and the lack I have won of
    the earth,

And the wrong amended by wrong, and the bitter wrong of my
  birth!"
She hath spread out her arms as she spake it, and away from the
  earth she leapt
And cut off her tide of returning; for the sea-waves over her swept,
40 And their will is her will henceforward; and who knoweth the
  deeps of the sea,
And the wealth of the bed of Gudrun, and the days that yet shall
  be?

* * *

Ye have heard of Sigurd aforetime, how the foes of God he slew;
How forth from the darksome desert the Gold of the Waters he
  drew;
How he wakened Love on the Mountain, and wakened Brynhild
  the Bright,
And dwelt upon Earth for a season, and shone in all men's sight.
Ye have heard of the Cloudy People, and the dimming of the day,
And the latter world's confusion, and Sigurd gone away;
Now ye know of the Need of the Niblungs and the end of broken
  troth,
All the death of kings and of kindreds and the Sorrow of Odin the
  Goth.

ALGERNON CHARLES SWINBURNE (1837–1909)

Sonnet: Between Two Seas

Everything about Swinburne and his poetry is extravagant, and only recently has he returned to critical favor. His faults are palpable: prolixity, sensationalism, narrow compass of concern, rush of sound over sense, repetitiveness. Yet he is a unique poet, a master of metric and of argument, and a Shelleyan intellectual skeptic whose polemic against Christianity is compelling.

His family background is incongruous with the man and his poetry. His father was an admiral in the British navy and his mother an earl's daughter. Raised on the Isle of Wight, he was early obsessed with the sea and the shoreline.

At Oxford, he studied classical literature and then left for London to begin a literary career. His alcoholism became legendary; his erotic life pivoted upon two French dominatrices who took turns whipping him soundly at their London establishment.

A close friend of Dante Gabriel Rossetti and George Meredith, Swinburne followed Rossetti's path of intoxication and collapsed at forty-two. He lived another thirty years, under the close supervision of a friend.

Swinburne was a brilliant critic, as in his books on William Shakespeare and on William Blake, and his early championing of Walt Whitman and of Charles Baudelaire. His scandalous *Poems and Ballads* (1866) first established his public, though subsequent volumes did little to widen his audience.

Among the uncollected poems, the *Sonnet: Between Two Seas* seems one of the last he wrote. The exhausted poet identifies himself with a wind-weary seabird. In his wish to pass with his song to the heaven of its desire and dread, he is not converting to the Christian divinity but reaffirming his lifelong, Shelleyan faith in the imagination.

Sonnet: Between Two Seas

Between two seas the sea-bird's wing makes halt
    Wind-weary; while with lifting head he waits
    For what may come of glory thro' the gates
That open still toward sunrise on the vault
High-domed of morning, & in flight's default
    With spreading sense of spirit anticipates
    What new sea now may lure beyond the straits
His wings exulting that her winds exalt
And fill them full as sails to seaward spread
10   Fulfilled with fair speed's promise. Pass, my song,
Forth to the heaven of thy desire & dread,
    The presence of our lord, long loved & long
Far off above beholden, who to thee
Was as light kindling all a windy sea.

THOMAS HARDY (1840–1928)

He Never Expected Much

Hardy was born on June 12, 1840, in the West Country he named Wessex in his novels. He studied architecture and arrived in London in 1862. For a quarter century he wrote novels (1871–1896) including *The Woodlanders, Far from the Madding Crowd, The Return of the Native, Tess of the d'Urbervilles,* and *The Mayor of Casterbridge.* In 1896, his final novel, *Jude the Obscure,* received so nasty a reception that he gave up novel writing for a return to poetry.

As a poet Hardy is a giant paradox, a Shelleyan High Romantic and one of the major poets of the twentieth century. From 1904 through 1908, he published a vast three-part lyrical drama, *The Dynasts,* on the Napoleonic Wars, very much in the mode of Shelley's *Prometheus Unbound. The Dynasts* is one of my personal favorites, yet fails with my students because of its length and because a verse novel now seems too archaic.

It is as a master of the short poem that Hardy continues to triumph. There are nine hundred poems in his collected edition, and perhaps a third are memorable and persuasive. One of these, given here, was composed on his eighty-sixth birthday, two years from his death. Stoic and resigned, it blends its cosmic doubts with the aesthetic dignity of considerable wisdom.

He Never Expected Much
[or]
A Consideration*

[A REFLECTION] ON MY EIGHTY-SIXTH BIRTHDAY

Well, World, you have kept faith with me,
    Kept faith with me;
Upon the whole you have proved to be
    Much as you said you were.
5   Since as a child I used to lie
Upon the leaze† and watch the sky,
Never, I own, expected I
    That life would all be fair.

'Twas then you said, and since have said,
10   Times since have said,
In that mysterious voice you shed
    From clouds and hills around:
"Many have loved me desperately,
Many with smooth serenity,
15 While some have shown contempt of me
    Till they dropped underground.

"I do not promise overmuch,
    Child; overmuch;
Just neutral-tinted haps‡ and such,"
20   You said to minds like mine.

---

*The title and subtitles reproduce the alternatives Hardy was considering when his death interrupted his revision of the manuscript.
†6: *leaze*: pasture (dialect)
‡19: *haps*: occurrences or accidents (archaic)

Wise warning for your credit's sake!
Which I for one failed not to take,
And hence could stem such strain and ache
    As each year might assign.

GERARD MANLEY HOPKINS (1844–1889)

To R.B.

Hopkins was born on July 28, 1844, at Stratford-in-Essex, the eldest of nine children of a very devout High Anglican, upper-middle-class household. He read classics at Balliol College, Oxford, where his tutor was the great, atheist literary critic, the Epicurean Walter Pater.

In March 1865, Hopkins befriended Digby Dolben, a promising young religious poet who died two years later, drowning at the age of nineteen. Whatever the relationship with Dolben had been, his death helped turn Hopkins away from erotic life. In 1866, Hopkins was converted to Roman Catholicism by John Henry Cardinal Newman. In 1868, he joined the Society of Jesus, and he remained under the discipline of the Jesuits until his death at forty-five. From 1884 to 1889, Hopkins was professor of Greek at the Catholic University in Dublin.

A poetic disciple of John Keats, Hopkins had a strongly ambivalent reaction to Walt Whitman. He judged Whitman to be "a very great scoundrel," an amazing reaction to the Ministering Angel of the Washington, DC, Civil War hospitals. But Hopkins also admitted a deep kinship with Whitman, whose celebration of homoeroticism must have alarmed the Jesuit priest-poet.

An experimenter in metric and diction, Hopkins remained unpublished until his friend Robert Bridges brought out a first edition of the poems in 1918.

Hopkins's last poem is his farewell sonnet to Bridges, composed in the Jesuit poet's final days. As a lament for the waste and loss of poetic genius, it beautifully belies itself, as it is one of his best. "Fathers" in the opening line is a verb, not a noun, meaning "begets," while "combs" in line 6 intimates that Hopkins's creative mind is like a mother caring for a child. Line 7 deliberately evokes Shelley's *Defense of Poetry,* where "the mind in creation is like a fading coal." Inspiration wanes but the mind brings forth what the insight fathered.

To R.B.

The fine delight that fathers thought; the strong
Spur, live and lancing like the blowpipe flame,
Breathes once and, quenchèd faster than it came,
Leaves yet the mind a mother of immortal song.

Nine months she then, nay years, nine years she long
Within her wears, bears, cares and combs the same:
The widow of an insight lost she lives, with aim
Now known and hand at work now never wrong.

Sweet fire the sire of muse, my soul needs this;
10   I want the one rapture of an inspiration
O then if in my lagging lines you miss

The roll, the rise, the carol, the creation,
My winter world, that scarcely breathes that bliss
Now, yields you, with some sighs, our explanation.

ROBERT BRIDGES (1844–1930)

Low Barometer

Bridges began as a medical doctor, but eventually devoted himself entirely to literature and became a remarkable lyric poet. *Low Barometer,* written late in his long career, is a skeptic's yielding to fundamental human fears of specters that haunt us all. "The baleful phantoms" are at once our repressed guilts and preternatural presences breaking through.

Low Barometer

The south-wind strengthens to a gale,
Across the moon the clouds fly fast,
The house is smitten as with a flail,
The chimney shudders to the blast.

On such a night, when Air has loosed
Its guardian grasp on blood and brain,
Old terrors then of god or ghost
Creep from their caves to life again;

And Reason kens he herits in
10   A haunted house. Tenants unknown
Assert their squalid lease of sin
With earlier title than his own.

Unbodied presences, the pack'd
Pollution and remorse of Time,
Slipp'd from oblivion reënact
The horrors of unhouseld crime.

Some men would quell the thing with prayer
Whose sightless footsteps pad the floor,
Whose fearful trespass mounts the stair
20   Or bursts the lock'd forbidden door.

Some have seen corpses long interr'd
Escape from hallowing control,
Pale charnel forms—nay ev'n have heard
The shrilling of a troubled soul,

That wanders till the dawn hath cross'd
The dolorous dark, or Earth hath wound
Closer her storm-spredd cloke, and thrust
The baleful phantoms underground.

ROBERT LOUIS STEVENSON (1850–1894)

Requiem

A dmirable storyteller, the Scottish romancer Stevenson, dead at forty-four of tuberculosis, always will be widely read throughout the world. Tales like *Kidnapped, Treasure Island,* and *Weir of Hermiston* are too enchanting not to prevail. As a poet, Stevenson chose to be deliberately minor.

Requiem

Under the wide and starry sky,
Dig the grave and let me lie.
Glad did I live and gladly die,
    And I laid me down with a will.

This be the verse you grave for me:
Here he lies where he longed to be;
Home is the sailor, home from sea,
    And the hunter home from the hill.

OSCAR WILDE (1854–1900)

From *The Ballad of Reading Gaol*

Wilde was a celebrity (and a scandal) in his own day, but is now appreciated as a canonical comic dramatist, particularly in *The Importance of Being Earnest.* He is a brilliant critical thinker in the tradition of his mentors, John Ruskin and Walter Pater. Three of his essays have influenced me profoundly: "The Critic as Artist," "The Soul of Man Under Socialism," and "The Decay of Lying."

His life was wonderful until he became a martyr, sentenced for homosexuality to Reading Gaol, where he suffered through two years of hard labor. He emerged broken and died in Paris at forty-six.

Except for *The Ballad of Reading Gaol,* written in France after his release, Wilde's poetry is weak and forgettable. His *Ballad* owes rather too much to Samuel Taylor Coleridge's *The Rime of the Ancient Mariner* but is rescued by its somber intensity.

From *The Ballad of Reading Gaol*

IV

There is no chapel on the day
    On which they hang a man:
The Chaplain's heart is far too sick.
    Or his face is far too wan,
280 Or there is that written in his eyes
    Which none should look upon.

So they kept us close till nigh on noon,
    And then they rang the bell,
And the Warders with their jingling keys
    Opened each listening cell,
And down the iron stair we tramped,
    Each from his separate Hell.

Out into God's sweet air we went,
    But not in wonted way,
290 For this man's face was white with fear,
    And that man's face was gray,
And I never saw sad men who looked
    So wistfully at the day.

I never saw sad men who looked
    With such a wistful eye
Upon that little tent of blue
    We prisoners called the sky,
And at every careless cloud that passed
299 In happy freedom by.

*   *   *

324 The Warders strutted up and down,
    And kept their herd of brutes,
Their uniforms were spick and span,
    And they wore their Sunday suits,
But we knew the work they had been at,
    By the quicklime on their boots.

330 For where a grave had opened wide,
    There was no grave at all:
Only a stretch of mud and sand
    By the hideous prison-wall,
And a little heap of burning lime,
335   That the man should have his pall.

*   *   *

348 For three long years they will not sow
    Or root or seedling there:
350 For three long years the unblessed spot
    Will sterile be and bare,
And look upon the wondering sky
    With unreproachful stare.

They think a murderer's heart would taint
    Each simple seed they sow.
It is not true! God's kindly earth
    Is kindlier than men know,
And the red rose would but blow more red,
    The white rose whiter blow.

A. E. HOUSMAN (1859–1936)

They Say My Verse Is Sad

I nfluenced by William Shakespeare's songs, the Border Ballads, and Heinrich Heine, Housman's poems are classical in mode: understated, pithy, firm in metric, and lucid in diction. He remains what he deserves to be, a popular poet of high aesthetic value.

Professor of Latin at Cambridge, Housman had published *A Shropshire Lad* in 1896, and did not bring out a second volume, *Last Poems,* until 1922. A posthumous volume, *More Poems,* did not add much to his achievement.

As an Oxford undergraduate, Housman evidently was in love with a fellow student who preferred marriage. The scar of the experience is evident throughout his poems.

More Poems leads off with *They Say My Verse Is Sad,* a fitting farewell for Housman.

They Say My Verse Is Sad

They say my verse is sad: no wonder;
    Its narrow measure spans
Tears of eternity, and sorrow,
    Not mine, but man's.

This is for all ill-treated fellows
    Unborn and unbegot,
For them to read when they're in trouble
    And I am not.

RUDYARD KIPLING (1865–1936)

The Fabulists

B orn in Bombay, Kipling was sent to school in England, where he was unhappy. He returned to India in 1882 and became a popular journalist, verse writer, and storyteller. He greatly admired Mark Twain, whose influence is apparent in *Kim,* Kipling's best novel.

After marrying an American, he lived with her in Vermont, but the marriage failed and he went back permanently to England. Prolific and versatile, he received the Nobel Prize in 1907.

A reaction against Kipling, by postcolonialist zealots and academic impostors, was very strong a generation ago, but seems now to have passed. What matters most are *Kim,* many grand short stories, and the verse.

I have chosen his most impressive poem, *The Fabulists,* which sums up his pragmatic and experiential wisdom. Late but not last, spiritually it is the last height Kipling attained. The refrains of the five stanzas lead to the final sadness, for a writer in particular, but also for everyone else. Our fables fail.

The Fabulists

When all the world would keep a matter hid,
    Since Truth is seldom friend to any crowd,
Men write in fable, as old Aesop did,
    Jesting at that which none will name aloud.
And this they needs must do, or it will fall
Unless they please they are not heard at all.

When desperate Folly daily laboureth
    To work confusion upon all we have,
When diligent Sloth demandeth Freedom's death,
10   And banded Fear commandeth Honour's grave—
Even in that certain hour before the fall,
Unless men please they are not heard at all.

Needs must all please, yet some not all for need,
    Needs must all toil, yet some not all for gain,
But that men taking pleasure may take heed,
    Whom present toil shall snatch from later pain.
Thus some have toiled but their reward was small
Since, though they pleased, they were not heard at all.

This was the lock that lay upon our lips,
20   This was the yoke that we have undergone,
Denying us all pleasant fellowships
    As in our time and generation.
Our pleasures unpursued age past recall.
And for our pains—we are not heard at all.

What man hears aught except the groaning guns?
　　What man heeds aught save what each instant brings?
When each man's life all imaged life outruns,
　　What man shall pleasure in imaginings?
So it hath fallen, as it was bound to fall,
30　We are not, nor we were not, heard at all.

Cuchulain Comforted

B y common consent the supreme Anglo-Irish poet and man of
letters, Yeats was for half a century the major continuator of
the English Romantic tradition, particularly of the visionary
poets William Blake and Percy Bysshe Shelley. As cofounder
and principal dramatist of Dublin's Abbey Theatre (Sean O'Casey and
John Millington Synge were among his discoveries), he had a lasting ef-
fect upon our idea of the post-Shakespearean play in English. Though
his theatrical career brought him the Nobel Prize, his greatness con-
denses itself into his extraordinary lyrical achievement.

I have discussed his last poems in this volume's introduction, reserv-
ing the most powerful, *Cuchulain Comforted,* for here. The "violent and
famous" Irish Achilles, Cuchulain long had been Yeats's archetypal vi-
sion of the hero. In his early (1895) group of poems, *The Rose,* Yeats in-
cluded *Cuchulain's Fight with the Sea,* where the hero hears "his own
name cried; / and fought with the invulnerable tide," in grief at having
slain his own son, not knowing the enemy's identity. In his very last play,
The Death of Cuchulain (1939), Yeats culminated a cycle of plays de-
voted to the Irish hero, including two superb dance dramas, *At the
Hawk's Well* and *The Only Jealousy of Emer.* Cuchulain is identified with

the sun and wins all the lunar women that Yeats himself failed to attain. But *The Death of Cuchulain* is an immensely bitter play, reflecting the dying Yeats's disdain for the decline of aristocratic values. The poet desires his hero to die badly and to no end: this is a Cuchulain indifferent to life and to death and to the passions for him manifested by an array of heroic women and goddesses. Yeats wants to reject the heroic as knowledge, but not as image, a complexity more beautifully developed in *Cuchulain Comforted.*

This inevitably phrased poem, one of Yeats's greatest, shockingly locates the most courageous of Irish mythological heroes among the cowards in the occult afterlife. When Yeats ends by chanting, of Cuchulain and the cowards, "They had changed their throats and had the throats of birds," he subtly modifies Dante's vision of his teacher Brunetto Latini, in the *Inferno,* who seems among the victorious and not among the defeated.

In Yeats's prose *A Vision,* you undergo a series of phases after you die, purging yourself for rebirth. The cowardly Shrouds, still afraid of the dead Cuchulain, are farther along in purgatorial process than the hero. All must live again, and they also fear the solitude of the soul's rebirth. The communal experience is as momentary in death as in life. The best commentary is Yeats's own in an earlier prose tract, *Per Amica Silentia Lunae:*

I shall find the dark grow luminous, the void fruitful, when I understand that I have nothing, that the ringers in the tower have appointed for the hymen of the soul a passing bell.

Cuchulain Comforted

A man that had six mortal wounds, a man
Violent and famous, strode among the dead;
Eyes stared out of the branches and were gone.

Then certain Shrouds that muttered head to head
Came and were gone. He leant upon a tree
As though to meditate on wounds and blood.

A Shroud that seemed to have authority
Among those bird-like things came, and let fall
A bundle of linen. Shrouds by two and three

10 Came creeping up because the man was still.
And thereupon that linen-carrier said:
"Your life can grow much sweeter if you will

Obey our ancient rule and make a shroud;
Mainly because of what we only know
The rattle of those arms makes us afraid.

We thread the needles' eyes, and all we do
All must together do." That done, the man
Took up the nearest and began to sew.*

"Now must we sing and sing the best we can,
20 But first you must be told our character:
Convicted cowards all, by kindred slain

---

*recalling a famous passage in *Inferno* XV: *e si ver noi aguzzecan le ciglia / come tecchio sartor fa nella cruna* ("and knitted their brows at us like an old tailor peering at his needle")

Or driven from home and left to die in fear."
They sang, but had nor human tunes nor words,
Though all was done in common as before,

They had changed their throats and had the throats of birds.

LIONEL JOHNSON (1867–1902)

The Dark Angel

The poetry of the 1890s is best represented by the young W. B. Yeats and by his friends, including Arthur Symons, Ernest Dowson, and the gifted but tormented Johnson.

Since his family's tradition was military, Johnson's break with his relatives was fourfold. He became a poet and critic, an Englishman backing Ireland's independence, an unwilling homosexual, and a Roman Catholic convert. He died at thirty-five of acute alcoholism.

The Dark Angel, his masterpiece, was composed in 1893, two years after his conversion. Johnson fuses his own other self, his homosexual desires, the Catholic Satan, and his precursors Percy Bysshe Shelley and Walter Pater into *The Dark Angel.* Shelley urged us to cast out remorse, powerfully castigating it as "the dark idolatry of self." Pater's "gem-like flame" transmutes into "flames of evil ecstasy." In the poem's closing two lines Johnson quotes Plotinus, founder of Neoplatonism, who chose "a flight of the alone to the alone," of the free spirit to the Divine.

The Dark Angel

Dark Angel, with thine aching lust
To rid the world of penitence:
Malicious Angel, who still dost
My soul such subtile violence!

Because of thee, no thought, no thing
Abides for me undesecrate:
Dark Angel, ever on the wing,
Who never reachest me too late!

When music sounds, then changest thou
Its silvery to a sultry fire:
Nor will thine envious heart allow
Delight untortured by desire.

Through thee, the gracious Muses turn
To Furies, O mine Enemy!
And all the things of beauty burn
With flames of evil ecstasy.

Because of thee, the land of dreams
Becomes a gathering-place of fears:
Until tormented slumber seems
One vehemence of useless tears.

When sunlight glows upon the flowers,
Or ripples down the dancing sea:
Thou, with thy troop of passionate powers,
Beleaguerest, bewilderest me.

Within the breath of autumn woods,
Within the winter silences:
Thy venomous spirit stirs and broods,
O master of impieties!

The ardour of red flames is thine,
30   And thine the steely soul of ice:
Thou poisonest the fair design
Of nature, with unfair device.

Apples of ashes, golden bright;
Waters of bitterness, how sweet!
O banquet of a foul delight,
Prepared by thee, dark Paraclete.

Thou art the whisper in the gloom,
The hinting tone, the haunting laugh:
Thou art the adorner of my tomb,
40   The minstrel of mine epitaph.

I fight thee, in the Holy Name!
Yet, what thou dost, is what God saith:
Tempter! should I escape thy flame,
Thou wilt have helped my soul from Death:

The second Death, that never dies,
That cannot die, when time is dead:
Live Death, wherein the lost soul cries,
Eternally uncomforted.

Dark Angel, with thine aching lust!
50   Of two defeats, of two despairs:

Less dread, a change to drifting dust,
Than thine eternity of cares.

Do what thou wilt, thou shalt not so,
Dark Angel! triumph over me:
Lonely, unto the Lone I go;
Divine, to the Divinity.

EDWIN ARLINGTON ROBINSON (1869–1935)

Why He Was There

One of the major American poets, now rather neglected, Robinson grew up in Maine, the landscape and social context of his earlier work. After two years at Harvard, he commenced a precarious career as a poet. Possibly because of his unrequited love for a sister-in-law, he never married.

Though he began to achieve some reputation for his poetry, he remained an unknown solitary (and heavy drinker) until President Theodore Roosevelt gave him a job (1905–1909) in the New York customhouse. Gradually his fame increased, in a life without event except for the frequent volumes he brought forth.

Like his friend Robert Frost, Robinson was deeply influenced by Ralph Waldo Emerson, particularly his late and mordant *The Conduct of Life*. A kind of stalwart melancholy emanates from the formal structures and moral restraints of Robinson's best poems.

Like Frost, Robinson could be a poet of hauntings. The sonnet *Why He Was There*, one of his final poems, is an oblique meditation upon death, our death. A lifelong friend reappears as a momentary presence, bound to vanish when Robinson departs. The title is splendidly ambiguous, since "He" can be both the dead friend and Robinson himself.

Why He Was There

Much as he left it when he went from us
Here was the room again where he had been
So long that something of him should be seen,
Or felt—and so it was. Incredulous,
I turned about, loath to be greeted thus,
And there he was in his old chair, serene
As ever, and as laconic and as lean
As when he lived, and as cadaverous.

Calm as he was of old when we were young,
10   He sat there gazing at the pallid flame
Before him. "And how far will this go on?"
I thought. He felt the failure of my tongue,
And smiled: "I was not here until you came;
And I shall not be here when you are gone."

Monsieur Qui Passe

B etter known in England than here, Mew is a considerable poet in the mode of Thomas Hardy, who aided her career. She came from an architect's family and lived in London for most of her life. Like her siblings, she suffered nervous disorders. After a breakdown in 1927, she killed herself the next year.

Mew had lesbian desires but apparently did not fulfill them, nor did she become Catholic, despite yearnings toward the Church. Her poems explore their self-dividings with extraordinary precision.

One of her last poems, published posthumously, *Monsieur Qui Passe*, seems to me her best. The title, locating us on the Seine, in Paris, has the vernacular meaning of "a ship passing in the night." The sense of lost opportunity is so subtly and sinuously conveyed that the poem becomes an elegy for Mew herself, for her partly unlived life.

Monsieur Qui Passe

QUAI VOLTAIRE

A purple blot* against the dead white door
In my friend's rooms, bathed in their vile pink light,
I had not noticed her before
She snatched my eyes and threw them back at me:
5   She did not speak till we came out into the night,
Paused at this bench beside the kiosk on the quay.
God knows precisely what she said—
I left to her the twisted skein,
Though here and there I caught a thread,—
10   Something, at first, about "the lamps along the Seine,
And Paris, with that witching card of Spring
Kept up her sleeve,—why you could see
The trick done on these freezing winter nights!
While half the kisses of the Quay—
15   Youth, hope,—the whole enchanted string
Of dreams hung on the Seine's long line of lights."

Then suddenly she stripped, the very skin
Came off her soul,—a mere girl† clings
Longer to some last rag, however thin,
20   When she has shown you—well—all sorts of things:
"If it were daylight—oh! one keeps one's head—
But fourteen years!—No one has ever guessed—
The whole thing starts when one gets to bed—
Death?—If the dead would tell us they had rest!
25   But your eyes held it as I stood there by the door—

*The title indicates that the speaker is a man. The *purple blot* is the woman of line 3.
†*a mere girl:* i.e., as opposed to a sexually experienced woman

One speaks to Christ—one tries to catch His garment's hem*—
One hardly says as much to Him—no more:
It was not you, it was your eyes—I spoke to them."

She stopped like a shot bird that flutters still,
30 And drops, and tries to run again, and swerves,
The tale should end in some walled house upon a hill.
My eyes, at least, won't play such havoc there,—
Or hers—But she had hair!—blood dipped in gold;
And here she left me throwing back the first odd stare.
35 Some sort of beauty once, but turning yellow, getting old.
Pouah! These women and their nerves!
God! but the night *is* cold!

*For the Christian imagery see Matthew 14:35–36 and especially 9:20–22: "a woman, which was diseased with an issue of blood twelve years, came behind [Jesus], and touched the hem of his garment. For she said within herself, If I may but touch his garment, I shall be whole. But Jesus turned him about: and when he saw her, he said. Daughter, be of good comfort; thy faith hath made thee whole. And the woman was made whole from that hour."

ROBERT FROST (1874–1963)

One More Brevity

F rost, in my view, disputes with Wallace Stevens, T. S. Eliot, and Hart Crane the aesthetic primacy among American poets of the twentieth century. Reading Crane, Frost remarked of poetry: "Why not have it imply everything?" His best works do.

By now Frost is American legend: a mountain in Vermont is named for him. His immense audience pleased him, but he had the wisdom not to write for it. Despite first impressions, he is a difficult poet, frequently not saying what more deeply he means.

Born in California, raised in New Hampshire, Frost made a lasting but difficult marriage with Elinor White, who died a quarter century before he did. Two of their children died in childhood. Of the other four, a daughter died young, another was placed in an institution, and a son killed himself.

A professed Emersonian, Frost shared the Concord sage's later nihilism.

This did not prevent his becoming our national poet, a unique role. His final volume, *In the Clearing* (1962), showed undiminished vigor.

I have chosen *One More Brevity* from among his last poems because it intends and achieves a final summing-up. Frost's star indeed was Sirius the dog star, and his poetry implies the following:

A meaning I was supposed to seek,
And finding, wasn't disposed to speak.

One More Brevity

I opened the door so my last look
Should be taken outside a house and book.
Before I gave up seeing and slept
I said I would see how Sirius kept
His watch-dog eye on what remained
To be gone into if not explained.
But scarcely was my door ajar,
When past the leg I thrust for bar
Slipped in to be my problem guest,
10   Not a heavenly dog made manifest,
But an earthly dog of the carriage breed;
Who, having failed of the modern speed,
Now asked asylum—and I was stirred
To be the one so dog-preferred.
He dumped himself like a bag of bones,
He sighed himself a couple of groans,
And head to tail then firmly curled
Like swearing off on the traffic world.
I set him water, I set him food,
20   He rolled an eye with gratitude
(Or merely manners it may have been),
But never so much as lifted chin.
His hard tail loudly smacked the floor
As if beseeching me, "Please, no more,
I can't explain—tonight at least."
His brow was perceptibly trouble-creased.
So I spoke in terms of adoption thus:
"Gustie, old boy, Dalmatian Gus,
You're right, there's nothing to discuss.
30   Don't try to tell me what's on your mind,

The sorrow of having been left behind,
Or the sorrow of having run away.
All that can wait for the light of day.
Meanwhile feel obligation-free.
Nobody has to confide in me."
'Twas too one-sided a dialogue,
And I wasn't sure I was talking dog.
I broke off baffled. But all the same
In fancy, I ratified his name,
40 Gustie, Dalmatian Gus, that is,
And started shaping my life to his,
Finding him in his right supplies
And sharing his miles of exercise.

Next morning the minute I was about
He was at the door to be let out
With an air that said, "I have paid my call.
You mustn't feel hurt if now I'm all
For getting back somewhere or further on."
I opened the door and he was gone.
50 I was to taste in little the grief
That comes of dogs' lives being so brief,
Only a fraction of ours at most.
He might have been the dream of a ghost
In spite of the way his tail had smacked
My floor so hard and matter-of-fact.
And things have been going so strangely since
I wouldn't be too hard to convince,
I might even claim, he was Sirius
(Think of presuming to call him Gus)
60 The star itself, Heaven's greatest start,
Not a meteorite, but an avatar,
Who had made an overnight descent

To show by deeds he didn't resent
My having depended on him so long,
And yet done nothing about it in song.
A symbol was all he could hope to convey,
An intimation, a shot of ray,
A meaning I was supposed to seek,
And finding, wasn't disposed to speak.

EDWARD THOMAS (1878–1917)

Liberty

T homas volunteered for the British army and died fighting in Flanders at thirty-nine. He and Robert Frost were close friends, and Frost encouraged him to start writing poetry in 1914. Until then Thomas had been a literary journeyman. In barely three years, Thomas composed a remarkable body of poems, fusing the modes of Thomas Hardy and of Frost.

Unlike Wilfred Owen and Isaac Rosenberg, Thomas is not a war poet but a writer of pastoral meditations, a lyrist of the open air.

With so little time, Thomas was not moved to write "last poems." I have chosen *Liberty,* long my favorite of all his work. It is a total vision of reality and the limitations imposed upon us all as we test our freedom. I brood endlessly in regard to the quietude of Thomas's wisdom:

> . . . There's none less free than who
> Does nothing and has nothing else to do,
> Being free only for what is not to his mind,
> And nothing is to his mind.

After this the poem's final four lines have a measured acceptance greatly, inevitably uttered, with an art difficult to equal. England lost what would have been a major poet in Edward Thomas.

Liberty

The last light has gone out of the world, except
This moonlight lying on the grass like frost
Beyond the brink of the tall elm's shadow,
It is as if everything else had slept
Many an age, unforgotten and lost—
The men that were, the things done, long ago,
All I have thought; and but the moon and I
Live yet and here stand idle over a grave
Where all is buried. Both have liberty
10   To dream what we could do if we were free
To do some thing we had desired long,
The moon and I. There's none less free than who
Does nothing and has nothing else to do,
Being free only for what is not to his mind,
And nothing is to his mind. If every hour
Like this one passing that I have spent among
The wiser others when I have forgot
To wonder whether I was free or not,
Were piled before me, and not lost behind,
20   And I could take and carry them away
I should be rich; or if I had the power
To wipe out every one and not again
Regret, I should be rich to be so poor.
And yet I still am half in love with pain,
With what is imperfect, with both tears and mirth,
With things that have an end, with life and earth,
And this moon that leaves me dark within the door.

ADELAIDE CRAPSEY (1878–1914)

The Lonely Death

B orn in Brooklyn Heights, New York, the daughter of a clergy-man, Adelaide Crapsey attended Vassar College. In 1906, her father was dismissed for heresy (actually left-wing political dissent) by the Episcopalian Church. A student of metrics, she taught poetics at Smith College, dying at thirty-six of tuberculosis.

Crapsey invented the cinquain, a five-line verse form with lines of two, four, six, eight, and two syllables. Her best work is in that form except for her resigned, haunting last poem, *The Lonely Death*.

The Lonely Death

In the cold I will rise, I will bathe
In waters of ice; myself
Will shiver, and shrive myself,
Alone in the dawn, and anoint
Forehead and feet and hands;
I will shutter the windows from light,
I will place in their sockets the four
Tall candles and set them a-flame
In the grey of the dawn; and myself
10   Will lay myself straight in my bed,
And draw the sheet under my chin.

WALLACE STEVENS (1879–1955)

Of Mere Being

Perhaps the greatest American poet since Walt Whitman and Emily Dickinson, Stevens had a legal career with a major Hartford, Connecticut, insurance company.

At Harvard, he studied with the philosopher poet George Santayana and wrote poetry, but gave it up until 1915, when he began to write the poems that would appear in *Harmonium* (1923), which vies with Hart Crane's *White Buildings* (1926) as the most outstanding first volume of American poetry since *Leaves of Grass* (1855).

Stevens married Elsie Moll in 1909 after a five-year courtship. Their daughter, Holly, an only child, was one of my closest friends, whom I continue to miss.

From 1923 through 1931, Stevens's poetry mysteriously ceased. The muse returned in early 1931, and continued with the poems of *Ideas of Order* (1936), *Parts of a World* (1942), and the crucial long poem *Notes Toward a Supreme Fiction* (1942). His best work came in the final phase: *Transport to Summer* (1947), *The Auroras of Autumn* (1951), and *Collected Poems* (1954).

Holly Stevens edited the best selected poems in her volume of his work, *The Palm at the End of the Mind,* the title being the first line of the last poem, *Of Mere Being,* written soon before Stevens went to the hospital to die.

A radiantly difficult poet, Stevens learned from Whitman the art of nuance, of what the later poet called: "The hum of thoughts evaded in the mind." That hum is heard in *Of Mere Being,* where "mere" means "pure." In his final vision, the dying poet beholds a phoenixlike bird in a palm tree precariously balanced at an edge and listens to its uninterpretable song. Yet he *sees* the bird fashioned (fangled) out of fire and intimates the final serenity of a great soul who has made friends with the necessity of dying.

Of Mere Being

The palm at the end of the mind,
Beyond the last thought, rises
In the bronze decor.

A gold-feathered bird
Sings in the palm, without human meaning,
Without human feeling, a foreign song.

You know then that it is not the reason
That makes us happy or unhappy.
The bird sings. Its feathers shine.

10   The palm stands on the edge of space.
The wind moves slowly in the branches.
The bird's fire-fangled feathers dangle down.

WILLIAM CARLOS WILLIAMS (1883–1963)

The World Contracted to a Recognizable Image

A n extraordinary extender of the American traditions of poetry, the superb innovator Williams was a lifelong pediatrician and obstetrician, delivering several generations of babies in Paterson, New Jersey.

Strongly influenced by John Keats and Walt Whitman, the ambitious Williams saw himself as being in poetic competition with Wallace Stevens, T. S. Eliot, and Hart Crane. His long poem *Paterson* (1946–1958) begins with a superb first book, but to me becomes problematic as it proceeds.

Williams may have been best at sequences, like the wonderful *Spring and All* (1923), but there also are scores of permanent lyric meditations.

The charming last poem, given here, has the delicacy and poignant precision of Williams at his most individual.

The World Contracted to a Recognizable Image

at the small end of an illness
there was a picture
probably Japanese
which filled my eye

an idiotic picture
except it was all I recognized
the wall lived for me in that picture
I clung to it as a fly

D. H. LAWRENCE (1885–1930)

Shadows

Lawrence, only now emerging from feminist censure, was a writer of world stature. He excelled at long and short stories, poems, polemics, prophecies, travel writing, criticism, and even at drama and history. His letters are endlessly absorbing; his religious stance was original and vitalizing. But he thought of himself primarily as a novelist and achieved magnificence in *The Rainbow* (1915) and *Women in Love* (1921).

Born in Nottinghamshire to a highly educated mother and a father who was a coal miner, Lawrence developed a fixation on his mother, the burden of his early, still very readable novel, *Sons and Lovers* (1913).

Lawrence attended Nottingham College, studying modern languages. One of his professors was married to the boisterous Frieda von Richthofen, who in May 1912 eloped with Lawrence to Germany and then on to Italy. The marriage to von Richthofen, stormy but sustaining, endured until Lawrence died of tuberculosis, aged forty-four.

As a novelist and story writer, Lawrence was in the tradition of the Brontës, George Eliot, and Thomas Hardy. In poetry he was influenced by Percy Bysshe Shelley and Hardy, but found himself more truly and more strange when he had absorbed Walt Whitman.

His last poem, *Shadows,* to me stands as one of the double handful of death poems in the language. It is a final hymn to an unknown, stranger god: grave, perfectly paced, ultimately hopeful of spiritual rebirth. Like Shelley, Hardy, and Whitman, the poet Lawrence was not a Christian but a seer of the invisible. I never get out of my memory the searing metaphor: "my wrists seem broken."

Shadows

And if tonight my soul may find her peace
in sleep, and sink in good oblivion,
and in the morning wake like a new-opened flower
then I have been dipped again in God, and new-created.
And if, as weeks go round, in the dark of the moon
my spirit darkens and goes out, and soft strange gloom
pervades my movements and my thoughts and words
then I shall know that I am walking still
with God, we are close together now the moon's in shadow.

10 And if, as autumn deepens and darkens
I feel the pain of falling leaves, and stems that break in storms
and trouble and dissolution and distress
and then the softness of deep shadows folding, folding
around my soul and spirit, around my lips
so sweet, like a swoon, or more like the drowse of a low, sad song
singing darker than the nightingale, on, on to the solstice
and the silence of short days, the silence of the year, the shadow,
then I shall know that my life is moving still
with the dark earth, and drenched
20 with the deep oblivion of earth's lapse and renewal.

And if, in the changing phases of man's life
I fall in sickness and in misery
my wrists seem broken and my heart seems dead
and strength is gone, and my life
is only the leavings of a life:

*　*　*

and still, among it all, snatches of lovely oblivion, and snatches of
   renewal
odd, wintry flowers upon the withered stem, yet new, strange
   flowers
such as my life has not brought forth before, new blossoms of me—

then I must know that still
I am in the hands [of] the unknown God,
he is breaking me down to his own oblivion
to send me forth on a new morning, a new man.

ELINOR WYLIE (1885–1928)

Ejaculation

A Shelleyan lyrist, beautiful and emotionally both volatile and fragile, Wylie was born into a diplomat's family. She married three times and wrote some effective novels, particularly *The Orphan Angel* (1926), a fictionalization of Percy Bysshe Shelley himself.

Her best volume now seems to me *Angels and Earthly Creatures* (1928), published after her death of a stroke, when she was just forty-three.

Wylie's metrical elegance fascinated the young James Merrill, who became the master poetic formalist of the second half of the twentieth century. *Ejaculation* serves as her last poem, gloriously defiant: "to tear / The living words from dying air."

Ejaculation

In this short interval to tear
The living words from dying air,
To pull them to me, quick and brave
As swordfish from a silver wave,
To drag them dripping, cold and salt
To suffocation in this vault
The which a lid of vapour shuts,
To shake them down like hazel-nuts
Or golden acorns from an oak
10   Whose twigs are flame above the smoke,
To snatch them suddenly from dust
Like apples flavoured with the frost
Of mountain valleys marble-cupped,
To leap to them and interrupt
Their flight that cleaves the atmosphere
As white and arrowy troops of deer
Divide the forest,—make my words
Like feathers torn from living birds!

ROBINSON JEFFERS (1887–1962)

I Have Been Warned

T he darkest poetic descendant of Walt Whitman, employing
Whitman's mode for a prophetic denunciation of American
vulgarity, Jeffers needs to be read very selectively. Spiritually
a child of Nietzsche, Jeffers has a measure of Lucretian
power, but he can fall into a noble monotony, like Swinburne at his rare
worst.

It is impressive that his life incarnated the myth of his poetry. Born
near Pittsburgh to a church organist mother and a father who was a pro-
fessor of the Old Testament, the young Jeffers studied ancient and mod-
ern languages. At the University of Southern California he met Mrs. Una
Call Kuster, with whom he shared a lifelong love affair. She and Jeffers,
after her divorce, married in 1913. They moved to Carmel, California,
where their twin sons were born in 1916. With the aid of masons, Jeffers
himself built the stone Tor House overlooking the Pacific. Later, Jeffers
constructed a stone tower dedicated to Una, whose death in 1950 left the
poet desolate during his final twelve years.

As a boy I read Jeffers and was swept away by his narrative strength in longer poems like *Tamar* and *Roan Stallion*. In my middle life, he wearied me, but in old age I have returned to him, admiring his negative energy as poet-prophet.

His last poem, given here, has an eloquent, plain decency as he defends his making "sacrifice / Of storied and imagined lives."

I Have Been Warned

I have been warned. It is more than thirty years since I wrote—
Thinking of the narrative poems I made, which always
Ended in blood and pain, though beautiful enough—my pain, my
   blood,
They were my creatures—I understood, and wrote to myself:
"Make sacrifices once a year to magic
Horror away from the house"—for that hangs imminent
Over all men and all houses—"This little house here
You have built over the ocean with your own hands
Beside the standing sea-boulders . . ." So I listened
To my Demon warning me that evil would come
If my work ceased, if I did not make sacrifice
Of storied and imagined lives, Tamar and Cawdor
And Thurso's wife—"imagined victims be our redeemers"—
At that time I was sure of my fates and felt
My poems guarding the house, well-made watchdogs
Ready to bite.

          But time sucks out the juice,
A man grows old and indolent.

T. S. ELIOT (1888–1965)

From *Little Gidding*

Thomas Stearns Eliot doubtless was the most famous and influential poet of the twentieth century. His aesthetic achievement in his best work clearly is permanent. As a literary critic, he was overpraised, while his cultural and religious polemics scarcely matter in the twenty-first century.

Born in St. Louis, Missouri, to a Unitarian family from New England, Eliot attended Harvard and then spent a year in Paris before proceeding to Oxford to study philosophy.

In 1915, he made the mistake of marrying Vivien Haigh-Wood, a disturbed and hysterical personality. From 1916 to 1925, Eliot worked at Lloyds Bank, London, but suffered a breakdown in 1921. His poetic reputation burgeoned with the publication of *The Waste Land* (1922). From 1925 on, Eliot worked as a publisher with Faber and Faber. In 1927, he became a British subject and was baptized into the Anglican Church. *Ash Wednesday* (1930) is the poem of his conversion.

In 1932, Eliot permanently separated from his wife, and after her death he married his secretary Valerie Fletcher in 1957 and enjoyed eight happy years with her until his death. He had received the Nobel Prize for literature in 1948.

Between 1935 and 1942, Eliot composed *Four Quartets,* a widely praised but uneven sequence. The last of them, *Little Gidding,* seems to me much the best, particularly Movement II, lines 80 through 151. For me (and others) they serve as Eliot's last poem, summing up much of his life and work.

Little Gidding is the name of a village not far from London where an Anglican community, both familial and monastic, was founded by Nicholas Ferrar in 1625. Cromwell's troops dispersed it during the civil wars, but it remained for Eliot the site of his pilgrimage.

An air-raid warden during the Battle of Britain from 1940 to 1941, Eliot experienced the night bombings and fire raids that greatly damaged London. This is the context of the second movement of *Little Gidding,* where the poet confronts an unlikely composite precursor, W. B. Yeats fused with Jonathan Swift, in the mode of Dante's *Inferno.* The time is the hallucinating glow of early morning, vividly conveyed by Eliot's blank *terza rima.* "Dark dove" refers to a German warplane, in a demonic parody of the Paraclete or comforter, the Holy Ghost descending as a fiery dove.

Eliot's "familiar compound ghost" alludes to William Shakespeare's "affable familiar ghost," the Rival Poet of Sonnet 86. Why Eliot invokes Yeats is an insoluble puzzle, unless the Irish Archpoet is a screen for the actual, still unacknowledged master, Whitman-Tennyson. *Inferno* XV describes Dante's encounter with his master, Brunetto Latini, a poet supposedly damned for homosexuality, which the actual historical figure never manifested. Whitman celebrates homoeroticism while Tennyson represses it, in palpable disregard of his lifetime's mourning for the early death of Hallam. Eliot, we learned recently, experienced a love relationship in Paris with a young French poet, Jean Verdenal, slain in World War I: "The awful daring of a moment's surrender / Which an age of prudence can never retract." By imputing to Brunetto Latini his own (presumably repressed) homoeroticism, Dante disguises elements in his true precursor, Virgil, who clearly was homosexual.

From line 131 onward ("Let me disclose the gifts reserved for age"), Eliot summons up an eloquence so pungent and purgatorial as to make this the finest passage that even he composed.

From *Little Gidding*

II

Ash on an old man's sleeve
Is all the ash the burnt roses leave.
Dust in the air suspended
Marks the place where a story ended.
Dust inbreathed was a house—
The wall, the wainscot and the mouse.
The death of hope and despair,
    This is the death of air.

There are flood and drouth
10   Over the eyes and in the mouth,
Dead water and dead sand
Contending for the upper hand.
The parched eviscerate soil
Gapes at the vanity of toil,
Laughs without mirth.
    This is the death of earth.

Water and fire succeed
The town, the pasture and the weed.
Water and fire deride
20   The sacrifice that we denied.
Water and fire shall rot
The marred foundations we forgot,
Of sanctuary and choir.
    This is the death of water and fire.

* * *

In the uncertain hour before the morning
    Near the ending of interminable night
    At the recurrent end of the unending
After the dark dove with the flickering tongue
    Had passed below the horizon of his homing
30 While the dead leaves still rattled on like tin
Over the asphalt where no other sound was
    Between three districts whence the smoke arose
    I met one walking, loitering and hurried
As if blown towards me like the metal leaves
    Before the urban dawn wind unresisting.
    And as I fixed upon the down-turned face
That pointed scrutiny with which we challenge
    The first-met stranger in the waning dusk
    I caught the sudden look of some dead master
40 Whom I had known, forgotten, half recalled
    Both one and many; in the brown baked features
    The eyes of a familiar compound ghost
Both intimate and unidentifiable.
    So I assumed a double part, and cried
    And heard another's voice cry: "What! are *you* here?"
Although we were not. I was still the same,
    Knowing myself yet being someone other—
    And he a face still forming; yet the words sufficed
To compel the recognition they preceded.
50 And so, compliant to the common wind,
    Too strange to each other for misunderstanding,
In concord at this intersection time
    Of meeting nowhere, no before and after,
    We trod the pavement in a dead patrol.
I said: "The wonder that I feel is easy,
    Yet ease is cause of wonder. Therefore speak:
    I may not comprehend, may not remember."

And he: "I am not eager to rehearse
My thoughts and theory which you have forgotten.
60 These things have served their purpose: let them be.
So with your own, and pray they be forgiven
By others, as I pray you to forgive
Both bad and good. Last season's fruit is eaten
And the fullfed beast shall kick the empty pail.
For last year's words belong to last year's language
And next year's words await another voice.
But, as the passage now presents no hindrance
To the spirit unappeased and peregrine
Between two worlds become much like each other,
70 So I find words I never thought to speak
In streets I never thought I should revisit
When I left my body on a distant shore.
Since our concern was speech, and speech impelled us
To purify the dialect of the tribe
And urge the mind to aftersight and foresight,
Let me disclose the gifts reserved for age
To set a crown upon your lifetime's effort.
First, the cold friction of expiring sense
Without enchantment, offering no promise
80 But bitter tastelessness of shadow fruit
As body and soul begin to fall asunder.
Second, the conscious impotence of rage
At human folly, and the laceration
Of laughter at what ceases to amuse.
And last, the rending pain of re-enactment
Of all that you have done, and been; the shame
Of motives late revealed, and the awareness
Of things ill done and done to others' harm
Which once you took for exercise of virtue.
90 Then fools' approval stings, and honour stains.

From wrong to wrong the exasperated spirit
    Proceeds, unless restored by that refining fire
    Where you must move in measure, like a dancer."
The day was breaking. In the disfigured street
    He left me, with a kind of valediction,
    And faded on the blowing of the horn.

CONRAD AIKEN (1889–1973)

Tetélestai

This fascinating American poet is now almost forgotten, a cultural loss I lament in my introduction to a recent, revised edition of his *Selected Poems* (2003).

Aiken was born in Savannah, Georgia, the oldest of four children. At eleven, he returned from school one day to discover the bodies of his parents. His father, a physician, had shot Aiken's mother and then himself. Adopted by an uncle in Cambridge, Massachusetts, Aiken was schooled there and went on to Harvard, where T. S. Eliot became a close friend.

Until he moved back to Savannah with his third wife, Aiken lived and wrote in London and on Cape Cod. He befriended and mentored Malcolm Lowry, whose *Under the Volcano* reflects Aiken's influence.

Aiken was a versatile author (poetry, novels, short stories, criticism, and autobiography); his chief guides were Sigmund Freud and James Joyce, who expressed an interest in his writing.

The poetry of Conrad Aiken is High Romantic in style, metric, and diction, richly opulent in verbal music, which displeases some critics. Profoundly nihilistic and Epicurean, Aiken had little patience for his friend T. S. Eliot's neo-Christianity or Ezra Pound's Fascism. As a humane skeptic, obsessed with mortality, he is extraordinarily sensitive to all the derangements of consciousness.

I have chosen *Tetélestai* as his last poem because it so perfectly exemplifies his stance and literary personality, though composed mid-career. The title, from the Greek New Testament, means "it is finished," the last word spoken by Christ on the cross.

Aiken's speaker is Everyman, already buried, contemplating mortality, and wistfully hopeful of somehow being remembered and saluted by "a fanfare of glory." This echoes Percy Bysshe Shelley's greater hope that his own *Ode to the West Wind* might prove to be "the trumpet of a prophecy" and Walt Whitman's outcry in *As I Ebb'd with the Ocean of Life:* "Just as much whence we come that blare of the cloudtrumpets."

Tetélestai

I

How shall we praise the magnificence of the dead,
The great man humbled, the haughty brought to dust?
Is there a horn we should not blow as proudly
For the meanest of us all, who creeps his days,
Guarding his heart from blows, to die obscurely?
I am no king, have laid no kingdoms waste,
Taken no princes captive, led no triumphs
Of weeping women through long walls of trumpets;
Say rather, I am no one, or an atom;
10 Say rather, two great gods, in a vault of starlight,
Play ponderingly at chess, and at the game's end
One of the pieces, shaken, falls to the floor
And runs to the darkest corner; and that piece
Forgotten there, left motionless, is I. . . .
Say that I have no name, no gifts, no power,
Am only one of millions, mostly silent;
One who came with eyes and hands and a heart,
Looked on beauty, and loved it, and then left it.
Say that the fates of time and space obscured me,
20 Led me a thousand ways to pain, bemused me,
Wrapped me in ugliness; and like great spiders
Dispatched me at their leisure. . . . Well, what then?
Should I not hear, as I lie down in dust,
The horns of glory blowing above my burial?

II

Morning and evening opened and closed above me:
Houses were built above me; trees let fall
Yellowing leaves upon me, hands of ghosts;

Rain has showered its arrows of silver upon me
Seeking my heart; winds have roared and tossed me;
30   Music in long blue waves of sound has borne me
A helpless weed to shores of unthought silence;
Time, above me, within me, crashed its gongs
Of terrible warning, sifting the dust of death;
And here I lie. Blow now your horns of glory
Harshly over my flesh, you trees, you waters!
You stars and suns, Canopus, Deneb, Rigel,
Let me, as I lie down, here in this dust,
Hear, far off, your whispered salutation!
Roar now above my decaying flesh, you winds,
40   Whirl out your earth-scents over this body, tell me
Of ferns and stagnant pools, wild roses, hillsides!
Anoint me, rain, let crash your silver arrows
On this hard flesh! I am the one who named you,
I lived in you, and now I die in you.
I your son, your daughter, treader of music,
Lie broken, conquered . . . Let me not fall in silence.

III

I, the restless one; the circler of circles;
Herdsman and roper of stars, who could not capture
The secret of self: I who was tyrant to weaklings,
50   Striker of children; destroyer of women; corrupter
Of innocent dreamers, and laugher at beauty; I,
Too easily brought to tears and weakness by music,
Baffled and broken by love, the helpless beholder
Of the war in my heart of desire with desire, the struggle
Of hatred with love, terror with hunger; I
Who laughed without knowing the cause of my laughter, who grew
Without wishing to grow, a servant to my own body;
Loved without reason the laughter and flesh of a woman,

Enduring such torments to find her! I who at last
60 Grow weaker, struggle more feebly, relent in my purpose,
Choose for my triumph an easier end, look backward
At earlier conquests: or, caught in the web, cry out
In a sudden and empty despair, "Tetélestai!"
Pity me, now! I, who was arrogant, beg you!
Tell me, as I lie down, that I was courageous.
Blow horns of victory now, as I reel and am vanquished.
Shatter the sky with trumpets above my grave.

     IV
. . . Look! this flesh how it crumbles to dust and is blown!
These bones, how they grind in the granite of frost and are nothing!
70 This skull, how it yawns for a flicker of time in the darkness,
Yet laughs not and sees not! It is crushed by a hammer of sunlight,
And the hands are destroyed. . . . Press down through the leaves of
     the jasmine,
Dig though the interlaced roots—nevermore will you find me;
I was no better than dust, yet you cannot replace me. . . .
Take the soft dust in your hand—does it stir: does it sing?
Has it lips and a heart? Does it open its eyes to the sun?
Does it run, does it dream, does it burn with a secret, or tremble
In terror of death? Or ache with tremendous decisions? . . .
Listen! . . . It says: "I lean by the river. The willows
80 Are yellowed with bud. White clouds roar up from the south
And darken the ripples: but they cannot darken my heart,
Nor the face like a star in my heart! . . . Rain falls on the water
And pelts it, and rings it with silver. The willow trees glisten.
The sparrows chirp under the eaves; but the face in my heart
Is a secret of music. . . . I wait in the rain and am silent."
Listen again! . . . It says: "I have worked, I am tired,
The pencil dulls in my hand: I see through the window
Walls upon walls of windows with faces behind them,

Smoke floating up to the sky, an ascension of sea-gulls.
90 I am tired. I have struggled in vain, my decision was fruitless,
Why then do I wait? with darkness, so easy, at hand! . . .
But tomorrow perhaps . . . I will wait and endure till
    tomorrow!" . . .
Or again: "It is dark. The decision is made. I am vanquished
By terror of life. The walls mount slowly about me
In coldness. I had not the courage. I was forsaken.
I cried out, was answered by silence . . . Tetélestai! . . ."

       V
Hear how it babbles!—Blow the dust out of your hand,
With its voices and visions, tread on it, forget it, turn homeward
With dreams in your brain. . . . This, then, is the humble, the
    nameless,—
100 The lover, the husband and father, the struggler with shadows,
The one who went down under shoutings of chaos, the weakling
Who cried his "forsaken!" like Christ on the darkening hilltop! . . .
This, then, is the one who implores, as he dwindles to silence,
A fanfare of glory. . . . And which of us dares to deny him?

ISAAC ROSENBERG (1890–1918)

A Worm Fed on the
Heart of Corinth

A
s with Edward Thomas and Wilfred Owen, Rosenberg's early death in battle during World War I deprived Britain of what would have been a major poet.

Rosenberg was born in Bristol of Eastern European Jewish emigrants. His parents moved to the London Jewish enclave in Whitechapel when he was seven. Like William Blake, he was apprenticed to an engraver, but at twenty-one a wealthier Jewish family began to subsidize his study of painting at the Slade School of Art. Some of his drawings and portraits are vivid and masterful, yet his poetic gifts were more remarkable.

From 1916, Rosenberg served as an enlisted man in trench warfare until he was killed in 1918.

Like Owen, Rosenberg was a disciple of John Keats. His Hebraic background emerges in a verse drama, *Moses,* and in prophetic fragments like the one I have chosen as a last poem, written about a year before his death. Blake would have loved this fragment, Keatsian yet biblical, with its warning that England could not heed. "This incestuous worm" is Satan, betrothed to England though not yet in possession of her. I admire particularly the series: "incestuous," "amorphous," "famous," "shadowless," and "amorous"—five attributes that fuse into a single identity.

A Worm Fed on the Heart of Corinth

A Worm fed on the heart of Corinth,
Babylon and Rome:
Not Paris raped tall Helen,
But this incestuous worm,
Who lured her vivid beauty
To his amorphous sleep.
England! famous as Helen
Is thy betrothal sung
To him the shadowless,
10   More amorous than Solomon.

SAMUEL GREENBERG (1893–1917)

To Dear Daniel

A painter-poet like Isaac Rosenberg, Greenberg had even less time, dying in a public hospital of tuberculosis at the age of twenty-three. Born in Vienna, Austria, the youngest of eight, he arrived with his family in New York City in 1900. A factory worker from thirteen on, he started to draw during visits to the Metropolitan Museum of Art. A critic, William Murrell Fisher, encouraged him. Tuberculosis consumed Greenberg during his last four years.

Fisher preserved the notebooks of autobiographical prose, drawings, and poetry. They were read by Hart Crane, who copied some of the poems out and wrote variations on them in his *Emblems of Conduct*.

A reader of Ralph Waldo Emerson, Greenberg was a Cranean poet before Crane. His postcard death poem, *To Dear Daniel*, is unlike most of his better work, since its lucid simplicity excludes the packed, dense texture and complex troping that excited Crane.

The pathos of Greenberg's brief life and impending death is prevented from complaint or oppressiveness by this poem's directness and dignity.

To Dear Daniel

There is a loud noise of Death
Where I lay;
There is a loud noise of life
Far away.

From low and weary stride
Have I flown;
From low and weary pride
I have grown.

What does it matter now
10   To you or me?
What does it matter now
To whom it be?

Again the stain has come
To me;
Again the stain has come
For thee.

WILFRED OWEN (1893–1918)

Futility

Born in Shropshire near the Welsh border, Owen came out of a Calvinist lower-middle-class family. Very close to his mother, he came to understand that his sexual orientation was homoerotic, but he seems to have evaded fulfilling his desires.

After some educational false starts, the young poet went to Bordeaux to teach English at a Berlitz school. He enlisted in 1915 and was sent to the western front as a lieutenant in January 1917. His descent into hell began almost immediately. Battle-weary, he was sent to Scotland to recuperate, and returned to action in August 1918. Known as a courageous officer, he received the Military Cross. A week before the armistice, Owen died in battle.

His best poems all date from August 1917 to September 1918 and are worthy of Keats, his poet of poets, being formal in design while loading every rift with ore. Frequently they employ what Owen called slant rhyme or pararhyme, a kind of consonance. Thus, in the great vision, *Strange Meeting,* Owen's rhymes include escaped/scooped, groined/groaned, bestirred/stared, and so on. Generally the second word's vowel is pitched lower than the first, so as to give a baffled effect, of expectation not being met.

Poets after Owen, particularly in the Auden generation, picked up Owen's device but without the subtle, downward modulation of vowel sounds. Owen's ironic indictments of the senseless slaughter on the western front were positively received by other poets, with the outrageous exception of the archpoet W. B. Yeats. An abstract celebrator of violence, though hardly a fighting man himself, Yeats angrily excluded Owen from *The Oxford Book of Modern Verse* (1936) on the grounds that "passive suffering" lacked aesthetic dignity. In a letter, Yeats became abusive on the subject, indicating anxiety on his part. Incredibly, he said that Owen's work was "unworthy of the poet's corner of a country newspaper," being "all blood, dirt and sucked sugar stick," "clumsy," and "discordant." The issue, I would think, is not between Owen, decorated for gallantry, and Yeats, resolved to keep safe, but between Yeats and Yeats. Ironically, Owen won in *that* contest when Yeats, in his last poem, *Cuchulain Comforted,* gives us Cuchulain accepting fellowship with cowards in the afterlife and employs Owen's pararhymes to give a proper sense of baffled expectations: man/gone, head/blood, shroud/afraid, fear/before. Yeats could have adopted this from Auden, but the lowering of vowel pitches suggests a subtly ironic amends on Yeats's part.

Futility was written in May 1918, half a year before Owen's death in battle. It shows utter mastery of pararhyme and total rejection of war and of Christianity alike. As in Keats, the earth is enough and the sun is god enough, and yet he is baffled by the futility of dying in warfare. "Fatuous sunbeams" is a masterstroke, worthy of continual meditation.

Futility

Move him into the sun—
Gently its touch awoke him once,
At home, whispering of fields unsown.
Always it woke him, even in France,
Until this morning and this snow.
If anything might rouse him now
The kind old sun will know.

Think how it wakes the seeds,—
Woke, once, the clays of a cold star.
10   Are limbs, so dear-achieved, are sides,
Full-nerved—still warm—too hard to stir?
Was it for this the clay grew tall?
—O what made fatuous sunbeams toil
To break earth's sleep at all?

LOUISE BOGAN (1897–1970)

The Dragonfly

I met with Bogan several times in the 1960s and learned much from arguing psychoanalysis with her. Though I expected we would talk about her poetry, upon which I was writing a brief commentary, she wished to discuss Freud and his therapy. I had sustained only a jot less than two years of analysis before my distinguished psychiatrist declined to go on, remarking that I was incapable of accepting my cure at the hands of another. Bogan had started psychoanalysis in her early twenties and kept at it for a half century until her death.

Born in Maine, she attended Boston University, married twice, and served as *The New Yorker*'s poetry editor for many years.

Her poetry, influenced most by Freud, Emily Dickinson, and W. B. Yeats, struggles to express a woman's consciousness, in the conviction that we still know very little about the very different ways that women and men love.

The Dragonfly, one of her last poems, may be her best. Since first reading it forty years ago, I cannot see a dragonfly floating on a pond without thinking of this firmly delicate lyric. Is it another of Bogan's lightly figured allegories of her own sense of being a woman resisting categorization by a male sensibility?

The Dragonfly

You are made of almost nothing
But of enough
To be great eyes
And diaphanous double vans;
To be ceaseless movement,
Unending hunger
Grappling love.

Link between water and air,
Earth repels you.
Light touches you only to shift into iridescence
Upon your body and wings.

Twice-born, predator,
You split into the heat.
Swift beyond calculation or capture
You dart into the shadow
Which consumes you.

You rocket into the day.
But at last, when the wind flattens the grasses,
For you, the design and purpose stop.

And you fall
With the other husks of summer.

Fish Food: An Obituary to Hart Crane

W heelwright, most Bostonian of Bostonians, had Colonial forebears and rarely left his native city, where at forty-three he was killed by a drunk driver. A choice of a last poem for him is difficult, but his superb elegy for his friend Hart Crane can be regarded as a self-elegy also.

Expelled from Harvard in 1920, the radical patrician Wheelwright studied architecture at MIT but showed little aptitude for its practice. His interests were poetry and Socialist politics. In 1937, the Socialists expelled him and his fellow Trotskyites. Wheelwright responded in 1938 by cofounding the Socialist Workers Party (Trotskyite), which still exists.

As an editor of the little magazine *Secession* in 1923, Wheelwright rather high-handedly printed *For the Marriage of Faustus and Helen,* Hart Crane's most ambitious poem to date, rewriting some of it without informing Crane. The quarrel and Crane's forgiveness are blended into *Fish Food,* which seems to me the most eloquent of all elegies by one American poet for another. There is an allusion to Crane's powerful poem, *The River,* from *The Bridge,* in the third stanza of Wheelwright's *Fish Food.* I think Crane would have greatly appreciated Wheelwright's gesture to the dead.

Fish Food: An Obituary to Hart Crane

As you drank deep as Thor, did you think of milk or wine?
Did you drink blood, while you drank the salt deep?
Or see through the film of light, that sharpened your rage with
    its stare,
a shark, dolphin, turtle? Did you not see the Cat
who, when Thor lifted her, unbased the cubic ground?
You would drain fathomless flagons to be slaked with vacuum—
The sea's teats have suckled you, and you are sunk far
in bubble-dreams, under swaying translucent vines
of thundering interior wonder. Eagles can never now
carry parts of your body, over cupped mountains
as emblems of their anger, embers to fire self-hate
to other wonders, unfolding white, flaming vistas.

Fishes now look upon you, with eyes which do not gossip.
Fishes are never shocked. Fishes will kiss you, each
fish tweak you; every kiss take bits of you away,
till your bones alone will roll, with the Gulf Stream's swell.
So has it been already, so have the carpers and puffers
nibbled your carcass of fame, each to his liking. Now
in tides of noon, the bones of your thought-suspended structures
gleam as you intended. Noon pulled your eyes with small
magnetic headaches; the will seeped from your blood. Seeds
of meaning popped from the pods of thought. And you fall.
    And the unseen
churn of Time changes the pearl-hued ocean;
like a pearl-shaped drop, in a huge water-clock
falling; from *came* to *go,* from *come* to *went.* And you fell.

* * *

Waters received you. Waters of our Birth in Death dissolve you.
Now you have willed it, may the Great Wash take you.
As the Mother-Lover takes your woe away, and cleansing
grief and you away, you sleep, you do not snore.
30 Lie still. Your rage is gone on a bright flood
away; as, when a bad friend held out his hand
you said, "Do not talk any more. I know you meant no harm."
What was the soil whence your anger sprang, who are deaf
as the stones to the whispering flight of the Mississippi's rivers?
What did you see as you fell? What did you hear as you sank?
Did it make you drunken with hearing?
I will not ask any more. You saw or heard no evil.

HART CRANE (1899–1932)

The Broken Tower

No other American poet was so preternaturally gifted as Hart Crane, who drowned himself at thirty-two, wrongly believing that his genius had forsaken him. His death poem, *The Broken Tower,* in itself demonstrates that his maturest work awaited him. In his despair, he truncated what should have been an achievement soaring beyond that of his acknowledged American precursors: Walt Whitman, Emily Dickinson, Herman Melville, T. S. Eliot, and Wallace Stevens.

Crane was born on July 21, 1899, in Garretsville, Ohio, the only child of Clarence Arthur Crane, a candy manufacturer (he invented Life Savers), and Grace Hart Crane, who suffered breakdowns.

Crane did not finish high school but educated himself by deep and wide reading. After his parents divorced in 1917, he was determined to become a poet. After an earlier sojourn in New York City, he returned there permanently in 1921, where he worked in advertising and then won patronage from Otto Kahn.

In the spring of 1924, Crane moved to Columbia Heights, Brooklyn, and lived in a room with a very close view of Brooklyn Bridge, the inspiration for his visionary epic, *The Bridge.*

Crane's first book, *White Buildings,* was published in 1926 and began to establish his reputation as a difficult but uniquely American poet, a celebratory yet tragic lyrist equal to Percy Bysshe Shelley, Arthur Rimbaud, Giacomo Leopardi, and John Keats.

Unable to sustain any profession but poetry, Crane suffered also by his inability to form a prolonged relationship with any of his many homosexual partners, even with the great love of his life, the Danish sailor Emil Oppfer, who inspired the extraordinary *Voyages* sequence of love poems. Alcoholism, long a problem, intensified the poet's unhappiness.

Most of *The Bridge* was written on the Isle of Pines in Cuba during 1926, on another grant from Otto Kahn. In part of 1929, Crane lived in Paris, the guest of Harry Crosby of the J. P. Morgan family. Crosby's Black Sun Press in Paris published the first edition of *The Bridge* in 1930. After the epic was published in New York City, to mixed reactions, Crane received a Guggenheim year in Mexico to write another long poem.

A bad year marked by serious drinking and little writing followed in Mexico. Toward the close of this broken interval, Crane began a surprising love affair with Peggy Cowley, estranged wife of his friend Malcolm Cowley. She is celebrated in *The Broken Tower* and sailed back to the United States with him in April 1932, when he chose to leap into the Caribbean.

The Broken Tower is both rhapsodic and difficult, partly because of its range of allusion: Herman Melville, W. B. Yeats, Walter Pater, Shelley, and Dante. Its stunning power transmutes Crane's agony into grand art, perhaps the Sublime of all American poetry. I think of it almost as the last poem to end all last poems.

The Broken Tower

The bell-rope that gathers God at dawn
Dispatches me as though I dropped down the knell
Of a spent day—to wander the cathedral lawn
From pit to crucifix, feet chill on steps from hell.

Have you not heard, have you not seen that corps
Of shadows in the tower, whose shoulders sway
Antiphonal carillons launched before
The stars are caught and hived in the sun's ray?

The bells, I say, the bells break down their tower;
10 And swing I know not where. Their tongues engrave
Membrane through marrow, my long-scattered score
Of broken intervals . . . And I, their sexton slave!

Oval encyclicals in canyons heaping
The impasse high with choir. Banked voices slain!
Pagodas, campaniles with reveilles outleaping—
O terraced echoes prostrate on the plain! . . .

And so it was I entered the broken world
To trace the visionary company of love, its voice
An instant in the wind (I know not whither hurled)
20 But not for long to hold each desperate choice.

My word I poured. But was it cognate, scored
Of that tribunal monarch of the air
Whose thigh embronzes earth, strikes crystal Word
In wounds pledged once to hope,—cleft to depair?

The steep encroachments of my blood left me
No answer (could blood hold such a lofty tower
As flings the question true?)—or is it she
Whose sweet mortality stirs latent power?—

And through whose pulse I hear, counting the strokes
30   My veins recall and add, revived and sure
The angelus of wars my chest evokes:
What I hold healed, original now, and pure . . .

And builds, within, a tower that is not stone
(Not stone can jacket heaven)—but slip
Of pebbles,—visible wings of silence sown
In azure circles, widening as they dip

The matrix of the heart, lift down the eye
That shrines the quiet lake and swells a tower . . .
The commodious, tall decorum of that sky
40   Unseals her earth, and lifts love in its shower.

STEVIE SMITH (1902–1971)

Black March

Born in Hull, Yorkshire, Florence Margaret Smith (always known as "Stevie") was moved to London when she was four, and lived in the family house in the suburb of Palmers Green her entire life. Her father was off in the British navy and her mother died early. Fortunately, Stevie had her "Lion Aunt" who raised her. In the wonderful film *Stevie,* the poet is played by Glenda Jackson, and the Lion Aunt by Mona Washburn, both very memorable, as is the anonymous reciter of Stevie's poems, Trevor Howard.

Her most famous poem, *Not Waving but Drowning,* retains its pungency, as do at least a score of others. Her true last poem, almost a death poem, *Black March,* moves with the metric of nursery rhyme or archaic popular song, which screens the very dark undersong. Rarely has the figure of death seemed so winsome and diffident as Stevie Smith's "old friend."

Black March

I have a friend
At the end
Of the world.
His name is a breath

5   Of fresh air.
He is dressed in
Grey chiffon. At least
I think it is chiffon.
It has a
10   Peculiar look, like smoke.

It wraps him round
It blows out of place
It conceals him
I have not seen his face.

15   But I have seen his eyes, they are
As pretty and bright
As raindrops on black twigs
In March, and heard him say:

I am a breath
20   Of fresh air for you, a change
By and by.

Black March I call him
Because of his eyes
Being like March raindrops
25   On black twigs.

(Such a pretty time when the sky
Behind black twigs can be seen
Stretched out in one
Uninterrupted
30   Cambridge blue* as cold as snow.)

But this friend
Whatever new names I give him
Is an old friend. He says:

Whatever names you give me
35   I am
A breath of fresh air,
A change for you

*Cambridge blue: light blue (the Cambridge university color in athletic contests with Oxford; Oxford's color being dark blue)

ROBERT PENN WARREN (1905–1989)

Heart of Autumn

I t is emotionally difficult to write about a deceased friend, even twenty years after his departure. I knew Warren only from 1973 on, and for most of fourteen years (until he became very ill) we lunched together every week at Yale, generally two-hour discussions that ended when I went off to teach and he to read and write at Yale's library.

I had converted to Warren's poetry with the publication of *Incarnations* (1968) and *Audubon* (1969). Until then the shadow of T. S. Eliot lingered upon Warren's poetry and inhibited him from developing a voice wholly his own. His great volumes seem to me *Or Else* (1974) and *Now and Then* (1978). By common consent, Warren's enduring novels are *All the King's Men* (1946) and *World Enough and Time* (1949).

Warren was born in Guthrie, Kentucky, and suffered a severe eye injury at sixteen; more than a decade later his left eye had to be removed. He attended Vanderbilt University, where the poet Allen Tate was his roommate and the poet John Crowe Ransom his teacher. All three also were to become distinguished literary critics of the Eliotic persuasion, the so-called New Critics.

Warren went on to further study at the University of California,

Berkeley. A first marriage failed, but eventually he married the writer Eleanor Clark, forming a lasting and happy relationship. Warren's first book was an attack on John Brown, the murderous martyr of abolitionism (1929). More than a half century later, Warren still fiercely denounced Ralph Waldo Emerson and Henry David Thoreau for encouraging and defending Brown, and delighted in telling me repeatedly that Emerson was the devil.

Warren's characteristic poem is an intensely dramatic lyric, frequently devoted to moral strife within the self. A powerful moralist, obsessed with St. Augustine's speculations on consciousness, time, and history, Warren nevertheless made clear to me his own refusal of any transcendental beliefs, including Christianity.

An unwilling sage, Warren necessarily was a wisdom writer, whether in verse or prose. His poetic eminence has not yet been absorbed, partly because he was so prolific, but also because he came between two generations of our poets. Robert Frost, Wallace Stevens, William Carlos Williams, T. S. Eliot, and Hart Crane were born between 1874 and 1899. W. H. Auden, Elizabeth Bishop, John Berryman, Randall Jarrell, Robert Lowell, Anthony Hecht, A. R. Ammons, James Merrill, and John Ashbery cover the span of birth dates from 1907 to 1927. Born in 1905, Warren was virtually a generation unto himself, and his poetic sea change in 1968 and 1969, when he individualized so remarkably in his sixties, was not widely noted or understood.

I have chosen *Heart of Autumn* as his last poem (in the sense that it speaks his total word, with permanent distinction) because I think he would have wished me to do so. I had written commentaries on it, and rather reluctantly he told me once that the poem might have been his best.

If there is an American Sublime—and I know, as a reader, that there is—Warren's *Heart of Autumn* is a vital strand in its litany.

Heart of Autumn

Wind finds the northwest gap, fall comes.
Today, under gray cloud-scud and over gray
Wind-flicker of forest, in perfect formation, wild geese
Head for a land of warm water, the *boom*, the lead pellet.

Some crumple in air, fall. Some stagger, recover control,
Then take the last glide for a far glint of water. None
Knows what has happened. Now, today, watching
How tirelessly *V* upon *V* arrows the season's logic,

Do I know my own story? At least, they know
10   When the hour comes for the great wing-beat. Sky-strider,
Star-strider—they rise, and the imperial utterance,
Which cries out for distance, quivers in the wheeling sky.

That much they know, and in their nature know
The path of pathlessness, with all the joy
Of destiny fulfilling its own name.
I have known time and distance, but not why I am here.

Path of logic, path of folly, all
The same—and I stand, my face lifted now skyward.
Hearing the high beat, my arms outstretched in the tingling
20   Process of transformation, and soon tough legs,

With folded feet, trail in the sounding vacuum of passage,
And my heart is impacted with a fierce impulse
To unwordable utterance—
Toward sunset, at a great height.

WILLIAM EMPSON (1906–1984)

Missing Dates

A major literary critic, Empson was a highly original but sparse poet. His bisexuality is the hidden burden of some of his strongest yet most obscure poems.

Born in Yorkshire, Empson attended Cambridge. At twenty-four, he published *Seven Types of Ambiguity,* still a critical work of interest. He taught in Tokyo from 1931 to 1934, and then published in 1935 both his *Poems* and *Some Versions of Pastoral.* From 1937 to 1939, he taught in Beijing; he then returned to England, where he finished a second volume of poems, *The Gathering Storm.* After the war, he taught in Beijing again until his final return home in 1952, then taught at Sheffield until he retired in 1971.

Empson sustained a complex marriage with a strong-minded wife, who allowed him relationships with her lovers. His intricate and perilous balance was maintained throughout a difficult and productive life.

Empson once told me that poetry had become "a mug's game" in which the next poem was a wager with the poet's ongoing life. On that basis, he had come late to an appreciation of Hart Crane. I have chosen *Missing Dates* even though it was written at the halfway point of his life. An inexorable death march, it attains perfection in its final quatrain, which Crane might have envied.

Missing Dates

Slowly the poison the whole blood stream fills.
It is not the effort nor the failure tires.
The waste remains, the waste remains and kills.

It is not your system or clear sight that mills
Down small to the consequence a life requires;
Slowly the poison the whole blood stream fills.

They bled an old dog dry yet the exchange rills
Of young dog blood gave but a month's desires;
The waste remains, the waste remains and kills.

10   It is the Chinese tombs and the slag hills
Usurp the soil, and not the soil retires.
Slowly the poison the whole blood stream fills.

Not to have fire is to be a skin that shrills.
The complete fire is death. From partial fires
The waste remains, the waste remains and kills.

It is the poems you have lost, the ills
From missing dates, at which the heart expires.
Slowly the poison the whole blood stream fills.
The waste remains, the waste remains and kills.

W. H. AUDEN (1907–1973)

A Lullaby

I always found Auden an endearing, humane personality, though I winced at his addressing me as "a dotty don." Talking about poetry to him distressed me, as he disliked my three favorites in the Lucretian tradition: Percy Bysshe Shelley, Walt Whitman, and Wallace Stevens. Once, when he had stayed overnight at my house, he insisted the next morning upon attending my Shelley seminar, during which he maintained a disbelieving silence.

While I admire Auden's songs and Byronic comic verse, I have problems with his devotional poems and reservations about his meditative mode, with its paradoxical distrust of art, despite its own high artistry.

Auden was born in York, England, to a medical family. At Oxford he published a first volume, and then went to Weimar, Germany, where he felt more freedom in his homosexuality. In 1937, he and Louis MacNeice published *Letters from Iceland*. He journeyed to the Spanish Civil War in 1937 and to China the next year. In January 1939, he left England for the United States, where he established a lasting relationship with Chester Kallman and became an American citizen in 1946. After that he divided his remaining years between New York City and Europe, dying in Vienna at sixty-six.

Prolific and versatile, Auden constantly wrote and published. and became the heir to T. S. Eliot, though happily free of Eliot's anti-Semitism, quasi-Fascism, and general contempt for the human condition.

In April 1972, a year before his death, Auden wrote a perfect elegy for himself in *A Lullaby*. Much that was best in the man and his work comes together here: moral courage, wit, compassion. Hastily (the Italian *frettolosamente*) the poet gets through his day, and lying down (jacent) in his bed enjoys the sensation of being a big baby again. Older than Auden was, I chant this lullaby to myself during sleepless nights and wish I had more of his admirable temperament.

A Lullaby

The din of work is subdued,
another day has westered
and mantling darkness arrived.
Peace! Peace! Devoid your portrait
5 of its vexations and rest.
Your daily round is done with,
you've gotten the garbage out,
answered some tiresome letters
and paid a bill by return,
10 all *frettolosamente.**
Now you have licence to lie,
naked, curled like a shrimplet,
jacent in bed, and enjoy
its cosy micro-climate:
15 *Sing, Big Baby, sing lullay.*

The old Greeks got it all wrong:
Narcissus† is an oldie,
tamed by time, released at last
from lust for other bodies,
20 rational and reconciled.
For many years you envied
the hirsute, the he-man type.
No longer: now you fondle
your almost feminine flesh
25 with mettled‡ satisfaction

---

*Lying down
†In Greek mythology, a beautiful youth who fell in love with his reflection in a stream and so pined away until be died.
‡High-spirited

imagining that you are
sinless and all-sufficient,
snug in the den of yourself,
Madonna and *Bambino*:*
30   *Sing, Big Baby, sing lullay.*

Let your last thinks all be thanks:
praise your parents who gave you
a Super-Ego† of strength
that saves you so much bother,
35   digit friends and dear them all,‡
then pay fair attribution
to your age, to having been
born when you were. In boyhood
you were permitted to meet
40   beautiful old contraptions,
soon to be banished from earth,
saddle-tank loks, beam-engines
and over-shot waterwheels.§
Yes, love, you have been lucky:
45   *Sing, Big Baby, sing lullay.*

Now for oblivion: let
the belly-mind take over
down below the diaphragm,
the domain of the Mothers,
50   They who guard the Sacred Gates,¶

*Madonna and child (Italian): used for the Virgin Mary and the baby Jesus
†Conscience (psychoanalysis)
‡Call them all "dear." *digit:* probably in the sense of counting
§Waterwheels with buckets on their rims that turn as the buckets fill with water. *saddle-tank loks:*
water tanks on the boilers of railway locomotives. *beam-engines:* parts of a steam engine
¶Perhaps the gates of ivory and horn in classical myth, through which false and true dreams, respec-
tivels, issued

without whose wordless warnings
soon the verbalising I
becomes a vicious despot,
lewd, incapable of love,
55   disdainful, status-hungry.
Should dreams haunt you, heed them not,
for all, both sweet and horrid,
are jokes in dubious taste,
too jejune to have truck with.
60   *Sleep, Big Baby, sleep your fill.*

LOUIS MACNEICE (1907–1963)

Charon

Born in Belfast, Northern Ireland, MacNeice came out of a Protestant Anglo-Irish family, son of a bishop of the established church. He attended Oxford, became a teacher of classics, married and divorced, and settled into a happy second marriage and a career of writing for the BBC. MacNeice died of pneumonia at sixty-five.

A skeptical wit, in life and in poetry, MacNeice is now somewhat neglected, but his poems are strong enough to survive.

Charon was written a year before MacNeice's unexpected death; the title is the name of the boatman who ferries dead souls to Hades, for the price of an obol each. The monosyllabic closing line clinches a perpetually surprising last poem.

Charon

The conductor's hands were black with money:
Hold on to your ticket, he said, the inspector's
Mind is black with suspicion, and hold on to
That dissolving map. We moved through London,
We could see the pigeons through the glass but failed
To hear their rumours of wars, we could see
The lost dog barking but never knew
That his bark was as shrill as a cock crowing,
We just jogged on, at each request
Stop there was a crowd of aggressively vacant
Faces, we just jogged on, eternity
Gave itself airs in revolving lights
And then we came to the Thames and all
The bridges were down, the further shore
Was lost in fog, so we asked the conductor
What we should do. He said: Take the ferry
Faute de mieux. We flicked the flashlight
And there was the ferryman just as Virgil
And Dante had seen him. He looked at us coldly
And his eyes were dead and his hands on the oar
Were black with obols and varicose veins
Marbled his calves and he said to us coldly:
If you want to die you will have to pay for it.

THEODORE ROETHKE (1908–1963)

In a Dark Time

Highly self-conscious, rarely free of ancestral voices (W. B. Yeats, T. S. Eliot, Walt Whitman, and Wallace Stevens), Roethke was an authentic poet who died too soon. Born and secluded in Michigan, he became a nature poet with a visionary difference. Tormented by insecurity and poetic desire, Roethke was a devoted teacher of other poets.

In a Dark Time, posthumously published, is the best among Roethke's last poems. Intense and formally wrought, it is an admirable work, though clearly still imbued by late Yeats.

In a Dark Time

In a dark time, the eye begins to see,
I meet my shadow in the deepening shade;
I hear my echo in the echoing wood—
A lord of nature weeping to a tree.
I live between the heron and the wren,
Beasts of the hill and serpents of the den.

What's madness but nobility of soul
At odds with circumstance? The day's on fire!
I know the purity of pure despair,
10   My shadow pinned against a sweating wall.
That place among the rocks—is it a cave,
Or winding path? The edge is what I have.

A steady storm of correspondences!
A night flowing with birds, a ragged moon,
And in broad day the midnight come again!
A man goes far to find out what he is—
Death of the self in a long, tearless night,
All natural shapes blazing unnatural light.

Dark, dark my light, and darker my desire.
20   My soul, like some heat-maddened summer fly,
Keeps buzzing at the sill. Which I is *I*?
A fallen man, I climb out of my fear.
The mind enters itself, and God the mind,
And one is One, free in the tearing wind.

To Walker Evans

Born in Knoxville, Tennessee, Agee went to Harvard and became a writer for *Fortune* and *Time* until 1948, when he became a masterly screenwriter. His scripts included *The African Queen* and *The Night of the Hunter*. In 1934, he published his earlier poems as *Permit Me Voyage,* the title an homage to Hart Crane. With Crane's friend the photographer Walker Evans, Agee composed *Let Us Now Praise Famous Men* (1941), an immensely moving vision of Alabama sharecroppers.

Agee died at just forty-five. His work includes a short novel *The Morning Watch* and the posthumously published *A Death in the Family.*

Had he lived, it seems probable that Agee would have developed his poetic gift. *To Walker Evans,* addressed to his friend and coauthor, is a last poem in the deep sense of a superb final statement, and to me is the best of Agee. It is also a better reading of Edgar's role and character in *King Lear* than any critic has accomplished. Archetype of the heroic survivor, Edgar, who is Gloucester's true son and Lear's godson, in his disguise as a madman avenges his father's eyes and his own outcast condition. The fiend, his enemy half brother Edmund, will go down in the duel with Edgar, but as Agee wisely sees, the play, in its highest sense, goes on showing us "the ruining heaven / Still captive the old wild king."

To Walker Evans

Against time and the damages of the brain
Sharpen and calibrate. Not yet in full,
Yet in some arbitrated part
Order the façade of the listless summer.

Spies, moving delicately among the enemy,
The younger sons, the fools,
Set somewhat aside the dialects and the stained skins of
    feigned madness,
Ambiguously signal, baffle, the eluded sentinel.

Edgar, weeping for pity, to the shelf of that sick bluff,
10 Bring your blind father, and describe a little;
Behold him, part wakened, fallen among field flowers shallow
But undisclosed, withdraw.

Not yet that naked hour when armed,
Disguise flung flat, squarely we challenge the fiend.
Still, comrade, the running of beasts and the ruining heaven
Still captive the old wild king.

ROBERT FITZGERALD (1910–1985)

Souls Lake

Educated at Harvard and Cambridge, Fitzgerald worked as a journalist and became a close friend of James Agee, whose poems he was to edit after Agee's death. After naval service, he taught and then lived and worked in Italy. From 1965 on, he was on the Harvard faculty. He is best known for his translations of *The Odyssey*, *The Iliad*, and *The Aeneid*.

A distinguished, rather classical poet, akin to Walter Savage Landor and to aspects of T. S. Eliot, Fitzgerald collected his poetry in *A Wreath for the Sea* (1943), *In the Rose of Time* (1956), and *Spring Shade* (1971).

Souls Lake seems to me Fitzgerald's central poem, a judgment he told me that he found acceptable. All of Fitzgerald is there: it is a majestic hymn to night, offers a stoic salute to mortality, and has a Lucretian sense of the Sublime. Something Virgilian emanates from it: an apprehension of suffering to come, but set aside for one beautiful night.

Souls Lake

The evergreen shadow and the pale magnolia
Stripping slowly to the air of May
Stood still in the night of the honey trees.
At rest above a star pool with my friends,
Beside that grove most fit for elegies,
I made my phrase to out-enchant the night.

The epithalamion, the hush were due,
For I had fasted and gone blind to see
What night might be beyond our passages;
10   Those stars so chevalier in fearful heaven
Could not but lay their steel aside and come
With a grave glitter into my low room.

Vague though the population of the earth
Lay stretched and dry below the cypresses,
It was not round-about but in my night,
Bone of my bone, as an old man would say;
And all its stone weighed my mortality;
The pool would be my body and my eyes,

The air my garment and material
20   Whereof that wateriness and mirror lived—
The colorable, meek and limpid world.
Though I had sworn my element alien
To the pure mind of night, the cold princes,
Behold them there, and both worlds were the same.

The heart's planet seemed not so lonely then,
Seeing what kin it found in that reclining.
And ah, though sweet the catch of your chorales,
I heard no singing there among my friends;
But still were the great waves, the lions shining,
30 And infinite still the discourse of the night.

Sonnet

Now widely accepted as a major American poet, Elizabeth Bishop was born in Worcester, Massachusetts. Her father died in 1911, and her mother was permanently institution-alized in 1916. The child was raised, in sequence, by her maternal grandparents in Nova Scotia, paternal grandparents in Worcester, and maternal aunt in Boston. From childhood on, she suffered from asthma. After graduating from Vassar in 1934, she went abroad until 1937. She met Marianne Moore and formed a permanent friendship that was a deep influence on Bishop's developing poetry. *North and South,* a superb first volume (1946), brought her the close friendship of Robert Lowell.

In 1951, Bishop began a long-lasting union with Lota de Macedo Soares. They lived together until Soares's suicide in 1967. Bishop remained in Brazil until 1970, by which time she had been recognized as a vital and important poet, particularly for *A Cold Spring* (1955) and *Questions of Travel* (1965).

Back in the United States, Bishop taught at Harvard and began a harmonious relationship with Alice Methfessel. In 1976, she published her last volume, *Geography III.* Death came three years later, depriving us of what could have been a major last phase. Since her death, critical esteem for Bishop has rightly increased. By any standards she is comparable to only the strongest American poets: Walt Whitman, Emily Dickinson, Robert Frost, Wallace Stevens, T. S. Eliot, William Carlos Williams, Marianne Moore, and Hart Crane.

I would like to represent Bishop here by her extraordinary early poem, *The Unbeliever,* which I persuaded her to recite as an extra work at the many readings where I introduced her. She finally rebelled and told an audience that while I liked the poem, she did not. I yield and print here what may have been her last poem, *Sonnet.* Sublimely truncated, a sonnet in fourteen lines, with only one to four words a line, this farewell takes one from "Caught" to "Freed" as the instruments break down and the mirror's dove (rainbow-bird, as at the end of Noah's flood) flies "wherever / it feels like, gay!" There is something of Dickinson in this glorious brief meditation, a perfect manifestation of Elizabeth Bishop's exacting art.

Sonnet

Caught—the bubble
in the spirit-level,
a creature divided;
and the compass needle
wobbling and wavering,
undecided.
Freed—the broken
thermometer's mercury
running away;
10   and the rainbow-bird
from the narrow bevel
of the empty mirror,
flying wherever
it feels like, gay!

JEAN GARRIGUE (1912–1972)

Grief Was to Go Out, Away

B orn in Evansville, Indiana, Garrigue studied at the University of Chicago and then at Iowa. She moved to New York City, where Delmore Schwartz showed good judgment in championing her poetry, then taken up by Marianne Moore.

Garrigue was early influenced by W. H. Auden and the very different Dylan Thomas, with whom her affinities were more authentic, since essentially she is a Keatsian poet and not a child of T. S. Eliot. Emily Dickinson also loved John Keats and shares with him Garrigue's poetic parentage.

I met Garrigue only once and came away with an impression of her troubled intensity, her air of seeking what never could be found by any of us. She tried to find a stable relationship with the volatile Josephine Herbst, a left-wing activist novelist, for whom she wrote *In Memory*, after Herbst's death in 1969.

Garrigue's posthumous volume, *Studies for an Actress* (1973), contains *Grief Was to Go Out, Away,* perhaps her last poem and certainly her best. Its genre is the American shore-ode, of which Walt Whitman was the inventor and many later American poets were the heirs, including Wallace Stevens, Hart Crane, Elizabeth Bishop, James Wright,

A. R. Ammons, and Amy Clampitt. Better than *In Memory,* this is her elegy for her relationship with Herbst and for herself, as she was to die just after her sixtieth birthday. So beautifully wrought is this last poem that I am left unhappy that Garrigue did not have a few more years to continue in this mode. She would now be remembered as someone close to an American Keats or a second Dickinson.

Grief Was to Go Out, Away

Grief was to go out, away
From this bedside of cliffs and shells,
Awakings in mornings to white-raged manes
Hoisting themselves up over rocks
And the white mother of foam sped
In a thickened broth curdled white
Back to the throngs of the oncoming rigors.

Grief was just in the having
Of so much heart pulse gone out and away
10 Into absence and the spent shadow
Of what ran from our fingers as ripples
Of shadow over the sand and what eluded
In a bending of mirrors the tipped tints and reflections
And was just so much running down the packed sands'
Mile-wide blondness of bird-tracked floor.

Was to behold in leaving, as if for the first time,
The fair-weathered crown of the mole
And the light chained to the grass-scattered peak.
Between the gates of the bullet-round rocks
20 Was to pluck up by the roots the salt hay
Where the seaweed lay wine red
And the foam was combed with gushed red
Was to leave carrying sealed in some envelope

Commandments instructing through leagues down
Where all must be seen through the hidden,
Through shade upon shade, down through layers,
Where all must be seen suspended in the stilled inner scene,

And the word must guard the deed and the inner word
Must not spill its center of smoke
30 Or break out from the windows of music
Playing deep in the night no one may arrive to

While you come back to your life
In a strange grace of gratitude,
Loving the least and most meagre
Of the held to, the unchosen given,
For here stand the encircling premises
By which don't they leap from, the distances?
And even as in the beat of the running foam
The enhalting power of the thing
40 Crowding the mind, pouring over the eyes?

Is it in the poignancy of tests
That we strike fire at the source,
At farewell that we clasp what we know,
And as if it were dying, run to embrace
Our life lying out there, misadventured, abstruse,
In the great wedge of light beamed forth—
Like messengers sallying out
To your "I see! I see!" bearing a scroll
On which the word is almost decipherable.

F. T. PRINCE (1912–2003)

Last Poem

P rince and I corresponded during his final ten years. Whether the subject was his own poetry—or William Shakespeare's, John Milton's, or Percy Bysshe Shelley's—his insights were continuous and illuminating.

Frank Templeton Prince, born in South Africa, studied at Balliol College, Oxford, and went to Princeton for graduate school. He served in British army intelligence in the Middle East during World War II. His teaching career at the University of Southampton was long and distinguished. It must have sorrowed Prince that he became known primarily for his remarkable war poem, *Soldiers Bathing.* His *Collected Poems, 1935–1992* is a richly varied volume.

A Roman Catholic convert, Prince was fascinated by Hasidism and wrote what I consider his most eloquent work, the sequence *Drypoints of the Hasidim* (1975), founding it upon the writings of Buber, Newman, Scholem, and Jacobs. These etchings of visionary writers are not inked in by Prince but are allowed a vivid eloquence in their very plainness. That is also the mode of Prince's *Last Poem.* Thomas Hardy gives Prince his *materia poetica,* which then is rendered as a drypoint in the second stanza.

Last Poem

Stand at the grave's head
Of any common
Man or woman,
Thomas Hardy said,
And in the silence
What they were,
Their life, becomes a poem.

And so with my dead,
As I know them
10   Now, in his
And her
Long silences;
And wait for, yet a while hence,
My own silence.

ROBERT HAYDEN (1913–1980)

Bone-Flower Elegy

ayden was the preeminent African-American poet before
our contemporaries Jay Wright, Thylias Moss, and Carl
Phillips. Clearly my criteria are purely aesthetic, and not
social or political.

Born in Detroit, Hayden attended Wayne State University. After
working for the Federal Writers' Projects, he went on to graduate study
at the University of Michigan. He was a convert to the Baha'i faith, and
many of his poems reflect its principles.

From 1969 on, Hayden was a professor at the University of Michi-
gan, where I met him when I lectured there. In conversation he was
courtly, gentle, and erudite: the poet and the man were one.

Hayden is best known for the sequences *Middle Passage* and *Runa-
gate Runagate,* both of them reflecting the influence of Hart Crane's
rhetorical art.

Bone-Flower Elegy is late Hayden, and essentially his last poem. As a
dream vision, it frees him from his lifetime evasion of homoerotic im-
pulses, incarnated by the beast angel who comes to rend and redeem the
poet, in a fearful Return of the Repressed.

Bone-Flower Elegy

In the dream I enter the house
    wander vast rooms that are
        catacombs midnight subway
           cavernous ruined movie-palace
        where presences in vulture masks
        play scenes of erotic violence
           on a scaffold stage   I want
      to stay and watch but know somehow
I must not linger and come to the funeral
10   chamber   in its icy nonlight see
        a naked corpse
           turning with sensual movements
          on its coffin-bed
      I have wept for you many times
      I whisper but shrink from the arms
        that would embrace me
          and treading water reach
    arched portals opening on a desert
groves of enormous nameless flowers
20   twist up from firegold sand
    skull flowers flowers of sawtooth bone
      their leaves and petals interlock
           caging me for you beastangel
          raging toward me
        angelbeast shining come
          to rend me and redeem

DELMORE SCHWARTZ (1913–1966)

The First Night of Fall and Falling Rain

D ead at fifty-two, Schwartz was the exemplary instance of poetic loss in his generation. Born in Brooklyn, he studied at NYU and Harvard. He made a Rimbaud-like advent with *In Dreams Begin Responsibilities* (1937), an inspired medley of verse and fictive prose. A number of volumes followed, culminating in *Summer Knowledge* (1959).

Schwartz left his teaching position at Syracuse in 1966, spent periods in a mental hospital, and then miserably died in a Times Square hotel.

A genuinely philosophical poet, Schwartz unfortunately was paranoid and hardly likely to survive in any literary world, which is agonistic by nature. His *Last and Lost Poems* (1979) show how much imaginative value was lost in his early decline and death. The poem given here I find very moving, as the shadow of an external world disturbs the poet's solipsistic consciousness.

The First Night of Fall and Falling Rain

The common rain had come again
Slanting and colorless, pale and anonymous,
Fainting falling in the first evening
Of the first perception of the actual fall,
The long and late light had slowly gathered up
A sooty wood of clouded sky, dim and distant more and more
Until, at dusk, the very sense of selfhood waned,
A weakening nothing halted, diminished or denied or set aside,
Neither tea, nor, after an hour, whiskey,
10   Ice and then a pleasant glow, a burning,
And the first leaping wood fire
Since a cold night in May, too long ago to be more than
Merely a cold and vivid memory.
Staring, empty, and without thought
Beyond the rising mists of the emotion of causeless sadness,
How suddenly all consciousness leaped in spontaneous gladness;
Knowing without thinking how the falling rain (outside, all over)
In slow sustained consistent vibration all over outside
Tapping window, streaking roof,
20   running down runnel and drain
Waking a sense, once more, of all that lived outside of us,
Beyond emotion, for beyond the swollen
            distorted shadows and lights
Of the toy town and the vanity fair
            of waking consciousness!

Space Walking

The Anglo-Welsh poet R. S. Thomas was born in Cardiff in 1913. He studied classics at the University of Wales, Bangor, and then theology. In 1936, he became a priest of the Anglican Church of Wales. A long and productive life ended peacefully in 2000.

His *Collected Later Poems, 1988–2000* shows him at full imaginative strength. Like Dylan Thomas, he was a High Romantic poet, but R.S. was far more Wordsworthian and less overtly experimental than the far more famous Dylan.

The last poem, *Space Walking,* I find immensely moving in its open skepticism yet still prevailing faith in confronting the gulf of death. As in Plato's *Atlantis* and Hart Crane's myth, the god is addressed as "the bridge builder." Anglican priest for more than sixty years, Thomas dismisses "the old stories" and yet hears the summons of the voice.

Space Walking

You, the bridge builder,
will you lay me down
a causeway between us
over the gulf I have come
to? What depths such as
the soul's, with yourself
always on the far
side? I have seen
my prayers fall one by one
into that chasm, and faith
was a plank too narrow
for me to tread. Walking
time's sea I have faltered
like Peter, unable
to believe you had arms
to sustain me. And now
the old stories are
done. There is no saviour
walking the waves. Matter
has become the physicist's
myth. Vertigo
is but the mind reeling
momentarily before its own
space. There is only
your voice now summoning
within interstices
of the machine not the flesh
but the spirit to launch
itself forth over the verbal deeps.

MAY SWENSON (1913–1989)

Staring at the Sea on the Day of the Death of Another

S wenson was born in Logan, Utah, to a Mormon family. After graduating from Utah State University she became a journalist. In 1936, Swenson moved to New York City in search of a poetic career: Though she always remained close to her family, a Mormon context was (and still is) uncomfortable for a lesbian.

Remarkably original and inventive from the start, her poetry quickly won admirers. From 1950 on, Swenson and Elizabeth Bishop became close friends. Swenson formed a lasting relationship with her companion, Rozanne Knudson, and lived with her in Sea Cliff, New York. Unfortunately there is still no *Collected Poems* of May Swenson, two decades after her death, and there is no single volume that is adequate to her achievement. *New and Selected Things Taking Place* (1978) was good up to its date, but the selected volume *Nature* (1994) is not useful enough. As of 2009, much of Swenson is not available.

Though Swenson, in my judgment, is fully comparable to Elizabeth Bishop, this shared eminence will not be clarified until all of Swenson's work is brought together. Ralph Waldo Emerson urged American poets to mount to Paradise by the stairway of surprise. After my half century of reading Swenson, she still surprises me.

One of Swenson's late poems, *Staring at the Sea on the Day of the Death of Another,* is an admirable last poem. It reflects powerfully upon the ways in which the death of a friend presages one's own.

Staring at the Sea on the Day
of the Death of Another

The long body of the water fills its hollow,
slowly rolls upon its side,
and in the swaddlings of the waves,
their shadowed hollows falling forward with the tide,

like folds of Grecian garments molded to cling
around some classic immemorial marble thing,
I see the vanished bodies of friends who have died.

Each form is furled into its hollow,
white in the dark curl,
10   the sea a mausoleum, with countless shelves,
cradling the prone effigies of our unearthly selves,

some of the hollows empty, long niches in the tide.
One of them is mine
and gliding forward, gaping wide.

DYLAN THOMAS (1914–1953)

Poem on His Birthday

Thisis the last poem Thomas composed before his death by alcohol in New York City, aged thirty-nine. His public readings had exhausted him.

Acclaimed in his lifetime, Thomas now is undervalued, dismissed as word-drunk or incoherent. Comparisons to Hart Crane are unfair to both poets but destructive to Thomas, who possessed neither Crane's uncanny logic of metaphor nor his Whitmanian ambition to renew a national myth. Thomas, less ambitious, set out resolutely to achieve his own voice while gladly accepting the influences of William Blake, D. H. Lawrence, John Keats, and the ultimate authority of William Shakespeare and the King James Bible. Whether he could be called a Christian poet is puzzling in regard to Thomas. His imagery is Christian, but he lacks specific faith.

Born in Wales, Thomas attended no university and began to write poetry at fifteen. In 1934, he moved to London and began to stir readers with his first book, *Eighteen Poems,* followed in 1936 by *Twenty-five Poems.* His career as a BBC broadcaster began in 1937, the year he married Caitlin MacNamara, with whom he was to have three children.

The Thomases were to live mostly in Wales with sojourns in London, Oxford, and Italy. Fame as a poet came in 1939 with *The Map of Love,* published in London, and *The World I Breathe,* in New York City.

From 1950 on, Thomas went on four reading tours in the United States, all to incessant public response, but so demanding that they were fueled by alcohol. Soon after the commencement of the fourth tour, the poet collapsed and died in New York City.

In May 1951, Thomas composed an elegiac villanelle for his father, who was to die a year later. "Do Not Go Gentle into That Good Night" has become proverbial, but I prefer the last-to-be-finished *Poem on His Birthday,* written in the summer of 1951, a few months from his unexpected death.

Poem on His Birthday

    In the mustardseed sun,
By full tilt river and switchback sea
    Where the cormorants scud,
In his house on stilts high among beaks
    And palavers of birds
This sandgrain day in the bent bay's grave
    He celebrates and spurns
His driftwood thirty-fifth wind turned age;
    Herons spire and spear.

10   Under and round him go
Flounders, gulls, on their cold, dying trails,
    Doing what they are told,
Curlews aloud in the congered waves
    Work at their ways to death,
And the rhymer in the long tongued room,
    Who tolls his birthday bell,
Toils towards the ambush of his wounds;
    Herons, steeple stemmed, bless.

    In the thistledown fall,
20 He sings towards anguish; finches fly
    In the claw tracks of hawks
On a seizing sky; small fishes glide
    Through wynds and shells of drowned
Ship towns to pastures of otters. He
    In his slant, racking house
And the hewn coils of his trade perceives
    Herons walk in their shroud,

The livelong river's robe
Of minnows wreathing around their prayer;
30   And far at sea he knows,
Who slaves to his crouched, eternal end
        Under a serpent cloud,
Dolphins dive in their turnturtle dust,
        The rippled seals streak down
To kill and their own tide daubing blood
        Slides good in the sleek mouth.

        In a cavernous, swung
Wave's silence, wept white angelus knells.
        Thirty-five bells sing struck
40   On skull and scar where his loves lie wrecked,
        Steered by the falling stars.
And tomorrow weeps in a blind cage
        Terror will rage apart
Before chains break to a hammer flame
        And love unbolts the dark

        And freely he goes lost
In the unknown, famous light of great
        And fabulous, dear God.
Dark is a way and light is a place,
50   Heaven that never was
Nor will be ever is always true,
        And, in that brambled void,
Plenty as blackberries in the woods
        The dead grow for His joy.

        There he might wander bare
With the spirits of the horseshoe bay
        Or the stars' seashore dead,

Marrow of eagles, the roots of whales
        And wishbones of wild geese,
60 With blessed, unborn God and His Ghost,
        And every soul His priest,
Gulled and chanter in young Haven's fold
        Be at cloud quaking peace,

        But dark is a long way.
He, on the earth of the night, alone
        With all the living, prays,
Who knows the rocketing wind will blow
        The bones out of the hills,
And the scythed boulders bleed, and the last
70   Rage shattered waters kick
Masts and fishes to the still quick stars,
        Faithlessly unto Him

        Who is the light of old
And air shaped Heaven where souls grow wild
        As horses in the foam:
Oh, let me midlife mourn by the shrined
        And druid heron's vows
The voyage to ruin I must run,
        Dawn ships clouted aground,
80 Yet, though I cry with tumbledown tongue,
        Count my blessings aloud:

        Four elements and five
Senses, and man a spirit in love
        Tangling through this spun slime
To his nimbus bell cool kingdom come
        And the lost, moonshine domes,
And the sea that hides his secret selves

Deep in its black, base bones,
Lulling of spheres in the seashell flesh,
90   And this last blessing most,

That the closer I move
To death, one man through his sundered hulks,
The louder the sun blooms
And the tusked, ramshackling sea exults;
And every wave of the way
And gale I tackle, the whole world then
With more triumphant faith
Than ever was since the world was said
Spins its morning of praise,

100   I hear the bouncing hills
Grow larked and greener at berry brown
Fall and the dew larks sing
Taller this thunderclap spring, and how
More spanned with angels ride
The mansouled fiery islands! Oh,
Holier then their eyes,
And my shining men no more alone
As I sail out to die.

JOHN BERRYMAN (1914–1972)

Henry's Understanding

Born in Oklahoma, the poet as a child suffered his father's suicide, a permanent trauma. Berryman attended Columbia University and Clare College, Cambridge. He taught at Harvard, Princeton, and finally at the University of Minnesota.

Married three times, Berryman was high-strung and difficult, an alcoholic and uneasily Roman Catholic. At fifty-seven, he leaped off a Minneapolis bridge to his death.

Berryman's early poetry curiously blends W. B. Yeats and W. H. Auden, yet his own characteristic voice emerged in his *Dream Songs,* both very funny and wildly despairing.

In 1972, he wrote his last poem, *Henry's Understanding,* in the form that makes it the coda to the *Dream Songs.* Remembering a prophetic moment a quarter century earlier, the poet anticipates his own impending suicide "into the terrible water."

I still admire Berryman's earlier poetry, but am divided on the *Dream Songs.* Yet many of them uncomfortably reside in my memory, including *Henry's Understanding.*

Henry's Understanding

He was reading late, at Richard's, down in Maine,
aged 32? Richard & Helen long in bed,
my good wife long in bed.
All I had to do was strip & get into my bed,
putting the marker in the book, & sleep,
& wake to a hot breakfast.

Off the coast was an island, P'tit Manaan,
the bluff from Richard's lawn was almost sheer.
A chill at four o'clock.
It only takes a few minutes to make a man.
A concentration upon now & here.
Suddenly, unlike Bach,

& horribly, unlike Bach, it occurred to me
that *one* night, instead of warm pajamas,
I'd take off all my clothes
& cross the damp cold lawn & down the bluff
into the terrible water & walk forever
under it out toward the island.

Thinking of the Lost World

I first became aware of Jarrell as a compassionate poet of World War II when as a teenager I read *Little Friend, Little Friend* (1945).

Jarrell was born in Nashville, Tennessee. He studied at Vanderbilt University and then taught at Kenyon College, befriending John Crowe Ransom and Robert Lowell.

From 1942 to 1945, Jarrell served in the Army Air Corps. He returned to teach at Sarah Lawrence College, and then at the University of North Carolina, Greensboro. In 1965, he deliberately walked out onto an interstate highway and was killed by a speeding car.

Influenced early by W. H. Auden, Jarrell in his poetic maturity turned to Robert Browning and reinvented the dramatic monologue by merging Browning with Marcel Proust.

In the year of his death, Jarrell wrote *Thinking of the Lost World,* pragmatically really his last poem. It is, to me, a lovely enigma why this elegy for the self concludes by asserting happiness.

Thinking of the Lost World

This spoonful of chocolate tapioca
Tastes like—like peanut butter, like the vanilla
Extract Mama told me not to drink.
Swallowing the spoonful, I have already traveled
5   Through time to my childhood. It puzzles me
That age is like it.
                    Come back to that calm country
Through which the stream of my life first meandred,
My wife, our cat, and I sit here and see
10   Squirrels quarreling in the feeder, a mockingbird
Copying our chipmunk, as our end copies
Its beginning.
                Back in Los Angeles, we missed
Los Angeles. The sunshine of the Land
15   Of Sunshine is a gray mist now, the atmosphere
Of some factory planet: when you stand and look
You see a block or two, and your eyes water.
The orange groves are all cut down . . . My bow
Is lost, all my arrows are lost or broken,
20   My knife is sunk in the eucalyptus tree
Too far for even Pop to get it out,
And the tree's sawed down. It and the stair-sticks
And the planks of the tree house are all firewood
Burned long ago; its gray smoke smells of Vicks.

25 *Twenty Years After,* thirty-five years after,
    Is as good as ever—better than ever,
    Now that D'Artagnan* is no longer old—
    Except that it is unbelievable.
    I say to my old self: "I believe. Help thou
30 Mine unbelief."†
                    I believe the dinosaur
    Or pterodactyl's married the pink sphinx
    And lives with those Indians in the undiscovered
    Country‡ between California and Arizona
35 That the mud girl told me she was princess of—
    Looking at me with the eyes of a lion,
    Big, golden. without human understanding,
    As she threw paper-wads from the back seat
    Of the car in which I drove her with her mother
40 From the jail in Waycross to the hospital
    In Daytona.§ If I took my eyes from the road
    And looked back into her eyes, the car would—I'd be—
    Or if only I could find a crystal set
    Sometimes, surely, I could still hear their chief
45 Reading to them from Dumas or *Amazing Stories;*¶
    If I could find in some Museum of Cars
    Mama's dark blue Buick, Lucky's electric,
    Couldn't I be driven there? Hold out to them
    The paraffin half picked out, Tawny's dewclaw—
50 And have walk to me from among their wigwams
    My tall brown aunt, to whisper to me: "Dead?

---

*The most daring of the musketeers in *The Three Musketeers* and its sequel, *Twenty Years After,* by Alexandre Dumas (1824–1895). French novelist and dramatist
†Spoken by the father of an epileptic child whom Jesus miraculously cured (Mark 9.24)
‡Cf. Shakespeare's *Hamlet* 3.1.81–82: "The undiscovered country from whose bourn no traveller returns"
§From a small town in southeastern Georgia to the east-central coast of Florida
¶A science fiction magazine of the 1940s

They told you I was dead?"

As if you could die!

If I never saw you, never again

55 Wrote to you, even, after a few years,

How often you've visited me, having put on,

As a mermaid puts on her sealskin, another face

And voice, that don't fool me for a minute—

That are yours for good . . . All of them are gone

60 Except for me; and for me nothing is gone—

The chicken's body is still going round

And round in widening circles, a satellite

From which, as the sun sets, the scientist bends

A look of evil on the unsuspecting earth.

65 Mama and Pop and Dandeen are still there

In the Gay Twenties.

The Gay Twenties! You say

The Gay Nineties . . . But it's all right: they *were* gay,

O so gay! A certain number of years after,

70 Any time is Gay, to the new ones who ask:

"Was that the first World War or the second?"

Moving between the first world and the second,

I hear a boy call, now that my beard's gray:

"Santa Claus! Hi, Santa Claus!" It *is* miraculous

75 To have the children call you Santa Claus.

I wave back. When my hand drops to the wheel,

It is brown and spotted, and its nails are ridged

Like Mama's. Where's my own hand? My smooth

White bitten-fingernailed one? I seem to see

80 A shape in tennis shoes and khaki riding-pants

Standing there empty-handed; I reach out to it

Empty-handed, my hand comes back empty,

And yet my emptiness is traded for its emptiness,

I have found that Lost World in the Lost and Found
85   Columns whose gray illegible advertisements
My soul has memorized world after world:
LOST—NOTHING. STRAYED FROM NOWHERE.
    NO REWARD.
I hold in my own hands, in happiness,
Nothing: the nothing for which there's no reward.

ROBERT LOWELL (1917–1977)

Epilogue

Rereading Lowell I have become confused, not by the poetry but by my own very mixed reaction. His first two volumes fascinated me but his move to "confessional poetry" in the late 1950s was not a fortunate development for his art. During the 1960s and 1970s my ambivalence was augmented, and in the decade after his death I gave up on him.

I was mistaken, as patient rereading has taught me. Like his friends John Berryman and Randall Jarrell, he survives his movement from one mannerism to another because his exacting art pivots upon a generous compassion.

Born in Boston to a patrician family, Lowell attended Harvard, Kenyon College, and Louisiana State, forming friendships with the poet critics John Crowe Ransom, Allen Tate, and R. P. Warren, and the critic Cleanth Brooks.

Lowell was married three times, to the writers Jean Stafford, Elizabeth Hardwick, and Caroline Blackwood. A manic-depressive, he was a purgatory for his wives. Converting to Roman Catholicism, he was a conscientious objector in World War II and was jailed for six months. He continued civil disobedience by protesting the Vietnam War.

The poignant *Epilogue* asks for too much, as Lowell surely knew. "Yet why not say what happened?" could lead to the death of art. Vermeer, master of illumination, is hardly similar to Lowell, but the poet's closing gesture disarms criticism.

Epilogue

Those blessèd structures, plot and rhyme—
why are they no help to me now
I want to make
something imagined, not recalled?
I hear the noise of my own voice:
The painter's vision is not a lens,
it trembles to caress the light.
But sometimes everything I write
with the threadbare art of my eye
10   seems a snapshot,
lurid, rapid, garish, grouped,
heightened from life,
yet paralyzed by fact.
All's misalliance.
Yet why not say what happened?
Pray for the grace and accuracy
Vermeer gave to the sun's illumination
stealing like the tide across a map
to his girl solid with yearning.
20   We are poor passing facts,
warned by that to give
each figure in the photograph
his living name.

W. S. GRAHAM (1918–1986)

Language Ah Now
You Have Me

G raham was born in Greenock, Scotland, and lived most of his life in Cornwall. A Late Romantic, influenced by Dylan Thomas, Hart Crane, and T. S. Eliot, Graham had an enthusiastic supporter in Eliot, who served as his editor and publisher.

Always going his own way, Graham suffered some early poverty but achieved reputation with *The Nightfishing* (1955), which seems to me a permanent longer poem or sequence. Rather than giving here one of his final works, I turn back to *Language Ah Now You Have Me* (1977).

Madron is the West Cornwall village where Graham lived. This rather Joycean poem, whimsical and difficult, builds on the jungle of metaphors ("mistakes in communication") to give a lasting vision of the entanglement of selfhood and language.

Language Ah Now You Have Me

1

Language ah now you have me. Night-time tongue,
Please speak for me between the social beasts
Which quick assail me. Here I am hiding in
The jungle of mistakes of communication.

I know about jungles. I know about unkempt places
Flying toward me when I am getting ready
To pull myself together and plot the place
To speak from. I am at the jungle face
Which is not easily yours. It is my home
10   Where pigmies hamstring Jumbo and the pleasure
Monkey is plucked from the tree. How pleased I am
To meet you reading and writing on damp paper
In the rain forest beside the Madron River.

2

Which is my home. The great and small breathers,
Experts of speaking, hang and slowly move
To say something or spring in the steaming air
Down to do the great white hunter for ever.

3

Do not disturb me now. I have to extract
A creature with its eggs between the words.
20   I have to seize it now, otherwise not only
My vanity will be appalled but my good cat
Will not look at me in the same way.

4

Is not to look. We are the ones hanging
On here and there, the dear word's edge wondering
If we are speaking clearly enough or if
The jungle's acoustics are at fault. Baboon,
My soul, is always ready to relinquish
The safe hold and leap on to nothing at all.
At least I hope so. Language now you have me
30 Trying to be myself but changed into
The wildebeest pursued or the leo pard
Running at stretch beside the Madron River.

5

Too much. I died. I forgot who I was and sent
My heart back with my bearers. How pleased I am
To find you here beside the Madron River
Wanting to be spoken to. It is my home
Where pigmies hamstring Jumbo and the pleasure
Monkey is plucked from the tree.

AMY CLAMPITT (1920–1994)

A Silence

B orn to a Quaker family in Iowa, Clampitt attended Grinnell College and worked for the National Audubon Society. Her splendid first volume of poems, *The Kingfisher,* was published when she was sixty-three. In her remaining decade she established a strong audience among discerning readers.

An American Romantic in direct touch with English precursors— William Wordsworth, John Keats, and Gerard Manley Hopkins— Clampitt in her late work became a major poet. Her superb last book, *A Silence Opens,* in its title poem culminates her preternaturally quiet meditative mysticism. Celebrating "a limitless / interiority," which opens to private revelation, Clampitt honors the martyred Mormon founder-charlatan and the imprisoned George Fox, founder of her own Quaker tradition.

A Silence

       past parentage or gender
       beyond sung vocables
       the slipped-between
       the so infinitesimal
       fault line
       a limitless
       interiority
       beyond the woven
       unicorn   the maiden
10   (man-carved   worm-eaten)
       God at her hip
       incipient
       the untransfigured
       cottontail
       bluebell and primrose
       growing wild   a strawberry
       chagrin   night terrors
       past the earthlit
       unearthly masquerade

20   (we shall be changed)

       a silence opens
               §
       the larval feeder
       naked   hairy   ravenous
       inventing from within
       itself its own
       raw stuffs'
       hooked silk-hung
       relinquishment

behind the mask
30 the milkfat   shivering
sinew   isinglass
uncrumpling   transient
greed to reinvest

§

names have been
given   (revelation
kif   nirvana
syncope)   for
whatever gift
unasked
40 gives birth to
torrents
fixities
reincarnations of
the angels
Joseph Smith
enduring
martyrdom

a cavernous
compunction driving
50 founder-charlatans
who saw in it
the infinite
love of God
and had
(George Fox
was one)
great openings

Aristocrats

D ouglas was the only British poet of World War II who had something of the distinction of Wilfred Owen and Isaac Rosenberg, both of whom died in World War I.

Educated at Merton College, Oxford, Douglas enlisted in 1940, became an officer in a tank regiment, and took part in the battle of El Alamein. Wounded and sent back to England for recovery, he was in the forces that invaded Normandy and died in battle three days after the landing.

Unlike Owen, and fighting in a just war, Douglas does not denounce warfare. He is almost dispassionate in his observation, as in the remarkable poem *Aristocrats* (1943), one of his finest. Celebrating the British aristocratic tradition, with its "stupidity and chivalry," Douglas tempers his praise with an edge of diffidence too subtle for any irony.

Aristocrats[*]

The noble horse with courage in his eye,
clean in the bone, looks up at a shellburst:
away fly the images of the shires[*]
but he puts the pipe back in his mouth.

5   Peter was unfortunately killed by an 88;[†]
it took his leg away, he died in the ambulance.
I saw him crawling on the sand, he said
It's most unfair, they've shot my foot off.

How can I live among this gentle
10   obsolescent breed of heroes, and not weep?
Unicorns, almost,
for they are fading into two legends
in which their stupidity and chivalry
are celebrated. Each, fool and hero, will be an immortal.

15   These plains were their cricket pitch[‡]
and in the mountains the tremendous drop fences[§]
brought down some of the runners. Here then
under the stones and earth they dispose themselves,
I think with their famous unconcern.
20   It is not gunfire I hear, but a hunting horn.

---

[*]*Aristocrats:* Earlier versions of Douglas's *Complete Poems* print a variant text entitled *Sportsmen.* "Lt Col. J. D. Player, killed in Tunisia. Enfidaville, Feb. 1943, left £3000 to the Beaufort hunt, and directed that the incumbent of the living in his gift should be 'a man who approves of hunting, shooting, and all manly spots, which are the backbone of the nation.'" (Douglas). Player actually died April 24, 1943.
[†]*88:* German tank armed with an 88-millimeter gun
[‡]*pitch:* playing field
[§]*drop fences:* fences in a steeplechase horserace

"The Darkness and the Light Are Both Alike to Thee"

A classical ironist and exquisite craftsman, Hecht has a voice like no other, not even his precursors W. H. Auden and John Crowe Ransom.

Born in New York City, Hecht attended Bard College and Columbia University. He entered the army in 1944 and served in Europe and Japan. A professor at Rochester and Georgetown, Hecht retired in 1993. His book on Auden's poetry is the best I know.

Like James Merrill in his own generation, Hecht was a major poet, renowned for his acute sensibility, total technical control, and compassionate wisdom.

His final volume, *The Darkness and the Light* (2001), concludes with this poem, the last poem in his last book.

"The Darkness and the Light
Are Both Alike to Thee"

Psalms 139:12

Like trailing silks, the light
Hangs in the olive trees
As the pale wine of day
Drains to its very lees:
Huge presences of gray
Rise up, and then it's night.

Distantly lights goon.
Scattered like fallen sparks
Bedded in peat, they seem
10   Set in the plushest darks
Until a timid gleam
Of matins turns them wan,

Like the elderly and frail
Who've lasted through the night,
Cold brows and silent lips,
For whom the rising light
Entails their own eclipse,
Brightening as they fail.

KENNETH KOCH (1925–2002)

Proverb

An adroit comedian of the spirit, Koch refreshes by vivacity, high good humor, and surrealistic jests. His truest precursor was John Dos Passos in the United States, and Koch can be credited for enriching poetic tradition by a prose sensibility, as Lord Byron did so magnificently. Koch's long baseball poem *Ko, or a Season on Earth* is Byronic throughout.

Koch also excelled in teaching poetry to children.

Proverb, almost his last poem, transforms the mode of elegy into something original, almost a new genre, a deceptively light farewell founded upon the full realization that life will go on without us.

Proverb

Les morts vont vite, the dead go fast, the next day absent!
Et les vivants sont dingues, the living are haywire.
Except for a few who grieve, life rapidly readjusts itself
The milliner trims the hat not thinking of the departed
The horse sweats and throws his stubborn rider to the earth
Uncaring if he has killed him or not
The thrown man rises. But now he knows that he is not going,
Not going fast, though he was close to having been gone.
The day after Caesar's death, there was a new, bustling Rome
10 The moment after the racehorse's death, a new one is sought for
    the stable
The second after a moth's death there are one or two hundred other
    moths
The month after Einstein's death the earth is inundated with new
    theories
Biographies are written to cover up the speed with which we go:
No more presence in the bedroom or waiting in the hall
Greeting to say hello with mixed emotions. The dead go quickly
Not knowing why they go or where they go. To die is human,
To come back divine. Roosevelt gives way to Truman
Suddenly in the empty White House a brave new voice resounds
And the wheelchaired captain has crossed the great divide.
20 Faster than memories, faster than old mythologies, faster than the
    speediest train.
Alexander of Macedon, on time!
Prudhomme on time, Gorbachev on time, the beloved and the lover
    on time!
Les morts vont vite. We living stand at the gate
And life goes on.

A. R. AMMONS (1926–2001)

In View of the Fact

Since his death it has become very difficult for me to write anything at all about the very great American poet Archie Randolph Ammons. One of my closest friends for a third of a century, he sustained me both personally and imaginatively. In retrospect, he seems to me to share the leadership of his rich generation of American poets with the visionary John Ashbery, with whom he exchanged a mutual aesthetic esteem.

Ammons was born in Whiteville, North Carolina, and attended Wake Forest College. He served in the navy in World War II, and afterward worked as an executive for a company manufacturing biological glass equipment.

A disciple of Ralph Waldo Emerson and Walt Whitman, Ammons gradually achieved poetic recognition, nationally and abroad. He taught at Cornell University, where he had a long and distinguished career.

Ammons's poetry is very extensive, ranging from really short poems to book-length works. His *Sphere* (1975) merits comparison to *Song of Myself*, and scores of his lyrics and meditations will prove imperishable.

In View of the Fact, composed five years before his death, seems to me truly his last poem. Firm and radiant, it is miraculous in its control of a universal poignance.

In View of the Fact

The people of my time are passing away: my
wife is baking for a funeral, a 60-year-old who

died suddenly, when the phone rings, and it's
Ruth we care so much about in intensive care:

it was once weddings that came so thick and
fast, and then, first babies, such a hullabaloo:

now, it's this that and the other and somebody
else gone or on the brink: well, we never

thought we would live forever (although we did)
10 and now it looks like we won't: some of us

are losing a leg to diabetes, some don't know
what they went downstairs for, some know that

a hired watchful person is around, some like
to touch the cane tip into something steady,

so nice: we have already lost so many,
brushed the loss of ourselves ourselves: our

address books for so long a slow scramble now
are palimpsests, scribble and scratches: our

index cards for Christmases, birthdays,
20 halloweens drop clean away into sympathies:

at the same time we are getting used to so
many leaving, we are hanging on with a grip

to the ones left: we are not giving up on the
congestive heart failures or brain tumors, on

the nice old men left in empty houses or on
the widows who decide to travel a lot: we

think the sun may shine someday when we'll
drink wine together and think of what used to

be: until we die we will remember every
30 single thing, recall every word, love every

loss: then we will, as we must, leave it to
others to love, love that can grow brighter

and deeper till the very end, gaining strength
and getting more precious all the way. . . .

JAMES MERRILL (1926–1995)

Days of 1994

Merrill was born in New York City, the son of the cofounder of Merrill Lynch, the brokerage company. After army service he graduated from Amherst and spent his time in travel, reading, and a long, marvelous career as a poet. To the intense sorrow of his many friends and admirers, he contracted AIDs and died at sixty-nine.

I have known only a few people so profoundly civilized and kind as Merrill. His lasting memorial is a body of major American poetry, as well as the Ingram Merrill Foundation, which supports painters and poets.

A Mozartian verse artist, Merrill surprised me and many others by *The Book of Ephraim* (1976), the first part of his visionary epic, *The Changing Light at Sandover*. Reflecting (and rebelling against) the influence of W. B. Yeats, *Sandover* is an occult splendor in which the spirit world and our reality so interpenetrate that a new reality is engendered.

Days of 1994 is a superbly conscious last poem in which the stricken Merrill serenely accepts his condition, ending with a line central to his life and work: "The laughter of old friends."

Days of 1994

These days in my friend's house
Light seeks me underground. To wake
Below the level of the lawn
—Half-basement cool through the worst heat—
Is strange and sweet.
High up, three window-slots, new slants on dawn:
Through misty greens and gilts
An infant sun totters on stilts of shade
Up toward the high
10   Mass of interwoven boughs,
While close against the triptych panes
Rock bears witness, Dragonfly
Shivers in place
Above tall Queen Anne's lace—
More figures from *The Book of Thel* by Blake
(Lilly & Worm, Cloudlet & Clod of Clay)
And none but drinks the dewy Manna in.

I shiver next, Light walking on my grave . . .
And sleep, and wake. This time, peer out
20   From just beneath the mirror of the lake
A gentle mile uphill.
Florets—the mountain laurel—float
Openmouthed, devout,
Set swaying by the wake of the flatboat:

Barcarole whose chords of gloom
Draw forth the youngest, purest, faithfullest,
Cool-crystal-casketed
Hands crossed on breast,

Pre-Raphaelite face radiant—and look,

30 Not dead, O never dead!
To wake, to wake
Among the flaming dowels of a tomb
Below the world, the thousand things
Here risen to if not above
Before day ends:
The spectacle, the book,
Forgetful lover and forgotten love,
Cobweb hung with trophy wings,
The fading trumpet of a car,

40 The knowing glance from star to star,
The laughter of old friends.

A Winter Daybreak
above Vence

Born to a working-class family in Martins Ferry, Ohio, Wright did his army service mostly in Japan. He went to Kenyon College to study with John Crowe Ransom, and then to Vienna on a Fulbright scholarship. A doctorate at the University of Washington brought him into contact with Theodore Roethke and helped confirm his vocation. After teaching at the University of Minnesota, he went on to Hunter College.

A first marriage ended in divorce, brought on by Wright's chronic depression and alcoholism, to be followed by a reasonably happy second union that ended only with his death.

Wright's early poems have the eloquent plainness of Edwin Arlington Robinson and Thomas Hardy. A surrealistic strain emerged in his translations of the major modern Austrian poet Georg Trakl, and reached imaginative splendor in Wright's finest volumes, *The Branch Will Not Break* and *Shall We Gather at the River,* where Walt Whitman is splendidly evoked. Only a few modern American poems are as eloquently compassionate as *The Minneapolis Poem* and *In Response to a Rumor That the Oldest Whorehouse in Wheeling, West Virginia, Has Been Condemned.* I remember telling Wright forty years ago how much I wished we had a foundation enlightened enough to sponsor sending him around to all the major American cities in order to write the definitive poem in dispraise of each.

The last poem in *Above the River,* Wright's complete poems (1990), is his vision of a winter dawn while he is gazing at the Mediterranean. In a final epiphany the poet discovers a new warmth in the self, warranted against skepticism by the realization "this is / The only life I have."

A Winter Daybreak above Vence

The night's drifts
Pile up below me and behind my back,
Slide down the hill, rise again, and build
Eerie little dunes on the roof of the house.
In the valley below me,
Miles between me and the town of St. Jeannet,
The road lamps glow.
They are so cold, they might as well be dark.
Trucks and cars
10 Cough and drone down there between the golden
Coffins of greenhouses, the startled squawk
Of a rooster claws heavily across
A grove, and drowns.
The gumming snarl of some grouchy dog sounds,
And a man bitterly shifts his broken gears.
True night still hangs on,
Mist cluttered with a racket of its own.

Now on the mountainside,
A little way downhill among turning rocks,
20 A square takes form in the side of a dim wall.
I hear a bucket rattle or something, tinny,
No other stirring behind the dim face
Of the goatherd's house. I imagine
His goats are still sleeping, dreaming
Of the fresh roses
Beyond the walls of the greenhouse below them
And of lettuce leaves opening in Tunisia.

* * *

I turn, and somehow
Impossibly hovering in the air over everything,
30   The Mediterranean, nearer to the moon
Than this mountain is,
Shines. A voice clearly
Tells me to snap out of it. Galway
Mutters out of the house and up the stone stairs
To start the motor. The moon and the stars
Suddenly flicker out, and the whole mountain
Apears, pale as a shell.

Look, the sea has not fallen and broken
Our heads. How can I feel so warm
40   Here in the dead center of January? I can
Scarcely believe it, and yet I have to, this is
The only life I have. I get up from the stone.
My body mumbles something unseemly
And follows me. Now we are all sitting here strangely
On top of the sunlight.

VICKI HEARNE (1946–2001)

News from the Dogs

A philosophical poet and by profession a horse and dog trainer, Hearne was a strong advocate of animal rights, particularly in her defense of the pit bull.

Born in Austin, Texas, Hearne studied at the University of California, Riverside, and began to train horses and dogs. She then studied at Stanford with the poet critic Donald Davie. Her first books, *Nervous Horses* and *In the Absence of Horses,* established her poetic originality. A prose work, *Adam's Task: Calling Animals by Name,* has been influential.

After teaching at Riverside, Hearne moved to Connecticut with her second husband and taught at Yale.

John Hollander edited *Tricks of the Light,* a comprehensive selection of Hearne's poetry (2007). The long title poem is her masterpiece, a post-Stevensian meditation on the limits of thought. Her last poem, *News from the Dogs,* seems to me Hearne at her extraordinary best: "There the dogs // Can always surprise the game / Bringing us news of ourselves."

News from the Dogs

The early gods say to cast
Slender and articulate
Visions out into the woods

And hope the dogs will follow
Through the fleeciest summer,
Returning with their mouths filled

With news we can make way for.
Instead, we raise gaudy flags
Into the treetops and teach

10   Our good red hound no more than
We know. The death of god casts
Shadows abroad. There the dogs

Can always surprise the game
Bringing us news of ourselves
If only we realize how

Deep the woods and dark the scent
As the bright season lengthens
Into the work of the mind for

Which the dogs live. God is born
20   Again in the news of death
So long as we let the dogs

Work in their way as we work
Our way back. How to fail: Cast
The dog at the tree you know

From childhood. Or cast the game
Yourself and instruct the dog
On his business, or cast off

The game in the wrong season
Or cast off the game. To fail
30   Is not to know that the game

For the dogs is what knowledge
Is when the world and the heart
Of a dog can dance out each
Moment in the mouth or cry
In the throat. In this season
Trees are flawless canopies.

Under them, no matter what
The outcomes, the dogs' return
Is the long scheduled event

40   Of warmth. Creatures foraging.
This is how we know the dogs
And all the other returns.

With Argos going ahead
Filled with immortality
As we are when the dogs show

The returns, the rocky quests,
To be names for each other,
The long truth of each other,

As though, at last, they were one.

AGHA SHAHID ALI (1949–2001)

The Veiled Suite

D ead before his fifty-second birthday, the Kashmiri-American poet Ali created in his poetry a unique blend of Shi'a Muslim Urdu literary modes with the elegant formalism of T. S. Eliot and James Merrill.

Born in New Delhi soon after the partition from Pakistan in which India held on to Muslim Kashmir, Ali studied at the University of Kashmir and then at Delhi before coming to America. He received a doctorate in literature at Pennsylvania State, and then taught at Hamilton College; at the University of Massachusetts, Amherst; and at the University of Utah.

Very close to his mother, Ali mourned her death in something close to a great elegy, *Lenox Hill*. Soon afterward, he too died, of brain cancer. He seems never to have formed a permanent relationship, except with her.

His collected poems, *The Veiled Suite,* appeared in 2009, eight years after his death. The title poem is his last and perhaps his strongest, a shapely canzone founded upon a personal dream of dying that is also an encounter with an erotic double. I can hear the influence of James Merrill but assimilated to Ali's own rich cultural heritage. It is one of the most haunting of all last poems.

The Veiled Suite

Faceless, he could represent only two alternatives:
that he was either a conscious agent of harm,
*or that he would unknowingly harm me anyway.**

"No mortal has or will ever lift my veil,"
he says. Strokes my arm. What poison is his eyes?
Make me now your veil, then see if you can veil
yourself from me. Where is he not from? Which vale
of tears? Am I awake? There is little sense
of whether I am his—or he is my—veil.
For, after the night is fog, who'll unveil
whom? Either he knows he is one with the night
or is unaware he's an agent of night—
10   nothing else is possible (who is whose veil?)
when he, random assassin sent by the sea,
is putting, and with no sense of urgency,

the final touches on—whose last fantasy?
Where isn't he from? He's brought the sky from Vail,
Colorado, and the Ganges from Varanasi
in a clay urn (his heart measures like the sea).
He's brought the desert too. It's deep in his eyes
when he says: "I want you to be mine alone, see."
What hasn't he planned? For music Debussy,
20   then a song from New Orleans in the *Crescent*'s
time nearing Penn Station. What's of the essence?
Not time, not time, no, not time. I can foresee

*From a dream in which I said this to myself (spring 2000)

he will lead each night from night into night.
I ask, "Can you promise me this much tonight:

that when you divide what remains of this night
it will be like a prophet once parted the sea.
But no one must die! For however this night
has been summoned, I, your mortal every night,
must become your veil . . . and I must lift your veil
30 when just one thing's left to consider: the night."
There's just one thing left to consider, the night
in which we will be left to realize
when the ice begins to break down in his eyes.
And the prophecies filming his gaze tonight?
What will be revealed? What stunning color sense
kept hidden so long in his eyes, what essence

of longing? He can kill me without a license.
The moon for its ivory scours the night.
Sent by the fog, he nearly empties in me all sense
40 of his gaze, till either he or I have lost all sense;
midnight polishes the remains of a galaxy.
What is left to polish now? What fluorescence?
Is there some hope of making a world of sense?
When I meet his gaze, there is again the veil.
On the farthest side of prophecy, I still need a veil.
Perhaps our only chance will be to ignite
the doom he sometimes veils in his eyes,
and the universe lost, like I am, in his eyes.

I wait for him to look straight into my eyes.
50 This is our only chance for magnificence.
If he, carefully, upon this hour of ice,

will let us almost completely crystallize,
tell me, who but I could chill his dreaming night.
Where he turns, what will not appear but my eyes?
Wherever he looks, the sky is only eyes.
Whatever news he has, it is of the sea.
But now is the time when I am to realize
our night cannot end completely with his eyes.
Something has happened now for me to prevail,
60   no matter what remains of this final night.

What arrangements haven't you made for tonight!
I am to hand you a knife from behind the veil
now rising quickly from your just-lit incense.
I'm still alive, alive to learn from your eyes
that I am become your veil and I am all you see.

(for Patricia O'Neill)

PERMISSIONS

1969, renewed 1997 by Mary von S. Jarrell. Reprinted by permission of Farrar, Straus and Giroux, LLC. Used by permission of Faber and Faber Ltd.

"I Have Been Warned" from *The Collected Poetry of Robinson Jeffers, Volume 3* by Robinson Jeffers, edited by Tim Hunt. Copyright © 1954, 1963 by Garth and Donnan Jeffers. Reprinted by permission of Stanford University Press.

"Proverb" from *Collected Poems of Kenneth Koch* by Kenneth Koch. Copyright © 2005 by The Kenneth Koch Literary Estate. Used by permission of Alfred A. Knopf, a division of Random House, Inc.

"Shadows" from *The Complete Poems of D. H. Lawrence* by D. H. Lawrence, edited by V. de Sola Pinto and F. W. Roberts. Copyright © 1964, 1971 by Angelo Ravagli and C. M. Weekley, Executors of the Estate of Frieda Lawrence Ravagli. Used by permission of Viking Penguin, a division of Penguin Group (USA) Inc.

"Epilogue" from *Collected Poems* by Robert Lowell. Copyright © 2003 by Harriet Lowell and Sheridan Lowell. Reprinted by permission of Farrar, Straus and Giroux, LLC.

"Charon" by Louis MacNeice, from *The Collected Poems*. Copyright © 1976. Reprinted by permission of Faber and Faber Ltd.

"Days of 1994" from *Collected Poems* by James Merrill, edited by J. D. McClatchy and Stephen Yenser. Copyright © 2001 by the Literary Estate of James Merrill at Washington University. Used by permission of Alfred A. Knopf, a division of Random House, Inc.

"Monsieur Qui Passe" from *Charlotte Mew: Collected Poems and Selected Prose* by Charlotte Mew. Copyright © 2003 by Charlotte Mew. Reprinted by permission of Carcanet Press Limited.

"Last Poem" from *Collected Poems: 1935–1992* by F. T. Prince, copyright © 1993 by F. T. Prince. Reprinted by permission of Sheep Meadow Press.

"In a Dark Time" from *Collected Poems of Theodore Roethke* by Theodore Roethke. Copyright © 1960 by Beatrice Roethke, Administratrix of the Estate of Theodore Roethke. Used by permission of Doubleday, a division of Random House, Inc.

"The First Night of Fall and Falling Rain" by Delmore Schwartz, from *Last and Lost Poems*. Copyright © 1962 The New York Times Company. Reprinted by permission of New Directions Publishing Corp.

"Black March" by Stevie Smith, from *Collected Poems of Stevie Smith*. Copyright © 1972 by Stevie Smith. Reprinted by permission of New Directions Publishing Corp.

"Of Mere Being" from *The Palm at the End of the Mind* by Wallace Stevens, edited by Holly Stevens. Copyright © 1967, 1969, 1971 by Holly Stevens. Used by permission of Alfred A. Knopf, a division of Random House, Inc.

"Staring at the Sea on the Day of the Death of Another" by May Swenson, from *Nature: Poems Old and New*. Copyright © The Literary Estate of May Swenson. Reprinted with permission of The Literary Estate of May Swenson. All rights reserved.

ACKNOWLEDGMENTS

I would like to thank my literary agents, Glen Hartley and Lynn Chu; my editor, Julia Cheiffetz; and my research assistant, Alice Steuart Hodgkins.

Harold Bloom is a Sterling Professor of Humanities at Yale University and a former Charles Eliot Norton Professor at Harvard. His more than twenty-five books include *The Best Poems of the English Language: From Chaucer Through Frost; Genius: A Mosaic of One Hundred Examplary Creative Minds; How to Read and Why; Shakespeare: The Invention of the Human; The Western Canon; The Book of J,* and *The Anxiety of Influence: A Theory of Poetry*. He is a MacArthur Prize Fellow, a member of the American Academy of Arts and Letters, and the recipient of many awards and honorary degrees, including the academy's Gold Medal for Belles Lettres and Criticism, the International Prize of Catalonia, and the Alfonso Reyes Prize of Mexico.